Central Health Studies
Consulting Editor: John Tingle

Patients' Rights, Responsibilities and the Nurse

Bridgit Dimond

Quay Publishing
BKT Information Services
CHS

Quay Publishing Ltd
7.1.9 Cameron House
White Cross, Lancaster LA1 4XQ

ISBN   1-85642-007-8

British Library Cataloguing-in-Publication Data

A catalogue record for this book is available from the British Library.

Designed and typeset by **BKT Information Services**, Nottingham, Specialists in Desktop Publishing, Database Development, and Electronic Media Publishing.

Printed in the United Kingdom by Bell and Bain Ltd., Glasgow

Contents

Acknowledgements

This book was developed from the inaugural lecture given at the Polytechnic of Wales (now the University of Glamorgan) on 24 March 1992. The author wishes to thank the many colleagues who assisted in the preparation of the paper. Special thanks are due to June Lewis, Gillian Reeve, Bette Griffiths, Tessa Shellens, and Jim Richardson for their invaluable assistance and suggestions.

Chapter 1:
Introduction

The term patient's rights appears to be of recent origin. Certainly the rights language associated with Thomas Paine and the social contract of Rousseau and John Locke was not concerned with the human being in sickness. Only recently has there been concern with the rights of the patient in relation to health care.

Codes of professional conduct have of course had a much longer history, for example the Hippocratic oath, but these have been couched in the language of the duties of the professional rather than in that of the rights of the patient.

In this country we do not have a Bill of Rights. There is no document which sets out fundamental inalienable rights of the people which the judges look to in deciding cases brought before the Courts. Instead if a person is claiming that the law recognises a particular right he must point to an Act of Parliament (i.e. a right given by Statute) or to a previous case where such a right was recognised by the judges in order to support his claim. If this cannot be established then there is a likelihood that the claim will be lost.

It is true that this country has been a signatory of the European Convention of Human Rights since 1951. However the Government has never accepted that the clauses in the Convention can be directly recognised by British judges. Any claimant has to take the case as far as he can within the English legal system and then, if he fails, he can then go to Strasbourg where the European Court of Human Rights sits. If he wins his case, there are no direct means of its findings being enforced in this country. All this can take an extremely long time—perhaps 6–7 years within our own judicial system and then a further eight years in Strasbourg. This can hardly meet the needs of justice. There is, therefore, at present discussion on whether this country should have a Bill of Rights, and leading figures both in the judiciary and also in the political arena are now discussing the possibility as by no means unwelcome or remote.

Why the preoccupation with the rights of the patient?

The recent emphasis on patients' rights can be seen to stem from two main sources. These are shown in figure 1(overleaf).

Raised expectations

As medical technology has advanced it is inevitable that this brings in its wake higher expectations of medicine, hospital care and the health professionals. In the nineteenth century, hospitals were places to avoid. Few would have a certainty of coming out alive. Yet now short stay for acute conditions has become almost part of our pattern of life. The

1

Figure 1.   Changing Attitudes to Health Care

1. **Rise in Expectations**
   - Advances in medical knowledge
   - Higher standard of living
   - Increased familiarity with health care and carers

2. **Concern at harmful effects of medical care**

establishment of the National Health Service within the Welfare State has crystallised these expectations in terms of the right to receive treatment without payment at the point of need.

Along with these expectations in relation to professional care, patients also expect higher standards in relation to the physical environment. Choice of menu is now routine. A high standard of furnishings and fittings is demanded. Even though there may still remain with us some hospitals and wards which reflect conditions of an earlier era, for the most part these are subject to planning proposals for refurbishment or replacement.

It is clear too that in the context of these higher expectations, patients are more likely to be prepared to voice their concerns and occasionally their complaints. In 1974, Community Health Councils were established with the function of bringing the consumer's views into the planning and provision of health care. They very quickly took on the role of assisting patients in bringing complaints and processing them. In the same year the office of the Health Service Commissioner was established (the Ombudsman). The function of this office is to investigate those complaints which the complainant considers still require further investigation even after the health authority has concluded its own investigation.

The procedures and organisations are therefore in place to facilitate the handling of complaints. Familiarity with the health scene and its employees perhaps makes it easier for patients to voice their concerns. The NHS is the largest employer in the country: there can be few who do not know someone employed by the NHS or who do not know someone who has been a patient. The preoccupation by the media, particularly television, with both fictional and non-fictional accounts of health care result in raised expectations for patients and these can be contrasted with the actual service provided. These expectations are then expressed in the language of rights.

Protection against health professionals

The second source of concern with patients' rights is of a very different nature. It stems from the work of such medical sociologists as Illich. He condemned the recent trend of medicalising human problems. Divorce, bereavement, redundancy, retirement, road traffic offences and similar causes of stress are treated as medical incidents and medication is prescribed. At the same time, increasing evidence of the harm and side effects of certain drugs has become available; patients are receiving treatment for the side effects of the drugs and sometimes for the side effects of those drugs prescribed to alleviate the side effects of the original drugs. This harm is known as iatrogenic illness. Patients need to know about such possibilities. They should be given such information before they consent to receiving treatment. Thus, there has been an emphasis on the protection of the patient and the patient's rights in relation to consent and to access to information.

This development has occurred over recent years and can be clearly seen in a comparison of the Mental Health Act of 1959 with that of 1983. See figure 2.

Figure 2: Comparison of Mental Health Acts of 1959 and 1983

	1959 Act		1983 Act
1.	Limited access to Mental Health Review Tribunal.	1.	Increased access to Mental Health Review Tribunal and automatic referral by managers.
2.	No regulations covering compulsory treatment.	2.	Part IV contains detailed provisions covering compulsory treatment.
3.	No statutory watchdog set up.	3.	Mental Health Act Commission established.

This latter Act shows a much stronger emphasis on the rights of the patient in terms of the information the patient should be given. Part 4 of the 1983 Act cover the provisions to be followed in the giving of treatment to detained patients, and if the patient is either incapable of giving consent or refuses to consent then treatment can only be given under clearly defined rules.

It is now interesting to note that new developments in medical technology are accompanied on the one hand by claims of entitlement and on the other by demands to protect those who may directly or indirectly suffer as a consequence: resuscitative medical technology has raised the issue of the right of patients to receive it as well as the right to die; *in vitro* fertilisation and related techniques have juxtaposed the claims of infertile couples against those of the embryo; in abortion the rights of the mother to have an abortion are balanced against the rights of the foetus; and in genetic engineering the rights of the congenitally disabled are contrasted with the concerns of those who seek to ban such work as being a slippery slope to a Brave New World.

What do we mean by rights?

Authors on the principles of Ethics have defined rights as:

> "In the tradition of liberal individualism, the language of rights has sometimes served as a means to oppose the status quo, to assert claims that demand recognition and respect and to force social reforms."

They define legal rights as 'claims that are justified by legal principles and rules' and moral rights as 'claims that are justified by moral principles and rules.' A moral right is a morally justified claim or entitlement.

In this book the concern is not to analyse the underlying ethical/moral basis of rights but to take several currently perceived rights which are relevant to the work of the nurse and analyse the extent to which they can be enforced by the patient and how they affect the work of the nurse. This is not to say that it is unimportant to have an understanding of the moral basis upon which rights are based or to appreciate the underlying ethical issues. These raise very important questions. However, there are several books which cover these topics and they are listed in the appendix.

Figure 3: Patient's Rights

1. A right to health care.

2. A right to a reasonable standard of care.

3. A right to consent.

4. A right of access to health records.

The rights which will be studied are set out in figure 3. They have been chosen because they figure prominently in the charters and the lists of rights published by charities and patients' associations. These organisations consider that if these rights are not yet recognised in law then the law should be changed to include them as legally enforceable rights.

Patients' Rights and the Practitioner

What is the practitioner's position in relation to those rights which are identified as having legal force?

She has a professional duty under the code of professional conduct to recognise and protect the rights of the patient. In this sense, she has an advocacy role in relation to the patient and certainly she might be involved in putting the patient's view to other professionals.

Difficulties however arise because there can be a conflict of rights and duties. The practitioner has a duty of care to the patient and yet the patient has a right of autonomy and it may be difficult for the practitioner to decide where her duty lies if there is an apparent clash.

For example, the practitioner may be caring for a person with learning disabilities who has limited capacity to make decisions. The client might have been given money and he may wish to spend it all on ice-creams and chocolates. The practitioner might decide that is not in his best interests and therefore try and limit his autonomy. This may seem a petty example to take but it is the same dilemma which exists in the case of deciding whether the patient should be resuscitated in circumstances where the patient has indicated that he does not wish it, but where the capacity of the patient to make that decision is doubted.

These dilemmas and the practitioner's accountability in relation to them will be considered in relation to each of the rights which will be covered in this book.

There are forms of accountability other than that of the profession and these together with the detail of the legal system and procedures and rules are set out in the author's earlier work.

Responsibilities of the Patient

There has been very little concern with the other side of the reciprocal relationship between patient and practitioner. Yet it is important to consider whether there are any enforceable duties which the patient owes to the practitioner. One chapter will therefore be devoted to a study of this. Again the emphasis will be on the legal basis of the patient's responsibilities. It will be found that whilst many may be considered to exist ethically or morally, few are recognised in law, especially in the National Health Service, where there is no contractual relationship between the patient and the service or its practitioners.

Questions and Exercises:

1. The book is concerned with legal rights. Are you aware of other rights which could not be enforced but which you consider should exist morally?

2. The concept of rights can be applied to other areas such as employment. Analyse your role as an employee and identify legal rights which you consider you possess as an employee. Can you identify the source of law which gives you these rights?

3. To what extent do you consider the nurse has a role to protect the rights of the patient? Are there others who are better suited to that task?

4. Have you encountered any schemes of patient advocacy? If so how effective were they in protecting the rights of the patient?

5. Do you think practitioners should consider that the patient has legal responsibilities towards those who care?

Chapter 2:
The Right to Medical Assistance & Health Care

This right must surely be one of the highest priorities in any civilised society. How far is this right enforceable by the patient? How far does our present law recognise this right of the individual and the reciprocal duty upon someone or some organisation to provide it?

Statutory Duties

To answer the question, we need to go back to the setting up of the National Health Service in 1948. Statutory duties were placed upon the Secretary of State, health authorities, social service authorities and general practitioners and other independent contractors such as dentists and pharmacists to carry out functions in relation to the provision of health care. The duties were subsequently re-enacted in the National Health Service Act 1977. The extensive provisions of the Act can be seen in figure 4 (overleaf).

The duties are comprehensive and extensive. However they are not absolute. Note the words which are italicised in figure 4. These words give considerable discretion to the Secretary of State and the health authorities.

Attempt to enforce statutory duties

The extent to which the duties are enforceable by a patient came before the courts in 1979. Orthopaedic patients at a hospital in Birmingham who had waited for treatment for periods longer than was medically advisable brought an action against the Secretary of State, the Regional Health Authority and the Area Health Authority. They were seeking a declaration that the Defendants were in breach of their duty under section 1 of the National Health Service Act 1977 to continue to promote a comprehensive health service designed to secure improvement in health and the prevention of illness. They also relied upon section 3, arguing that the defendants were in breach of their duties to provide accommodation, facilities and services for those purposes.

The judge however held that it was not for the courts to direct parliament as to what funds to make available to the health service and how to allocate them. The Secretary of State's duties under section 3 to provide services 'to such extent as he considers necessary', gave him discretion as to the disposition of financial resources. The court could only interfere if the Secretary of State acted so as to frustrate the policy of the Act or as no reasonable Minister could have acted. No such breach had been shown in the present case. The application was dismissed against all

7

Figure 4: Statutory Duties of the Secretary of State

Section 1(1)   It is the Secretary of State's duty to continue the promotion in England and Wales of a comprehensive health service designed to secure improvement

a.   in the physical and mental health of the people of those countries, and

b.   in the prevention, diagnosis and treatment of illness, and for the purpose to provide or secure the effective provision of services in accordance with this Act.

Section 3(1)   It is the Secretary of State's duty to provide throughout England and Wales, *to such extent as he considers necessary to meet all reasonable requirements*:

a.   hospital accommodation

b.   other accommodation for the purpose of any service provided under this Act;

c.   medical, dental, nursing and ambulance services;

d.   such other facilities for the care of expectant and nursing mothers and young children as he considers are appropriate as part of the health service;

e.   such facilities for the prevention of illness, the care of persons suffering from illness and the after-care of persons who have suffered from illness as he considers are appropriate as part of the health service;

f.   such other services as are required for the diagnosis and treatment of illness.

the Defendants. (*R. v. Secretary of State for Social Services,* ex parte *Hincks*, 1979)

Heart-baby case

The reasoning was confirmed in a more recent case.

Mrs. Walker's son required a heart operation and was on the waiting list. A date was fixed for the operation to be performed but was postponed by the Birmingham Health Authority. She applied to the court for a judicial review of the decision by the Health Authority. The High Court judge refused her application. She appealed to the Court of Appeal who upheld the earlier decision. The court held that it was not for the court to substitute its own judgement for that of those responsible for the allocation of resources. It would only interfere if there had been a failure to allocate funds in a way which was unreasonable or where there had been breaches of public duty. (In re Walker's application, 1987)

The refusal to grant Mrs. Walker's application is understandable. Resources are finite; demand for health care infinite.

How does this affect the nurse practitioner?

It means that in the unequal equation of demand and supply she would have a legal duty to ensure that priorities are determined reasonably. There may well be occasions when patients are refused admission because of an absence of resources. She should ensure that her managers are aware of any deficiencies in resources and such shortages are constantly monitored. Such shortages do not provide a defence for any negligence or professional misconduct on her part. (As will be seen in the next section, the patient is entitled to receive the appropriate standard of care.) However, if the priorities are reasonably determined, the patient could not bring a successful action against the nurse or authority.

The case of Baby J. (1991)

A recent case has shone a new light onto this issue. The doctors responsible for the care of a severely brain-damaged baby refused to put him on a ventilator. The baby (known as Baby J.) had suffered severe injuries in an accident at home when 8 weeks old. At the time of the court hearing he was 16 months and was being cared for by foster parents. He had become blind, was paralysed, suffered from epilepsy and had to be fed by a tube. The doctors considered that placing him on a ventilator would cause him additional distress and pain. The mother brought an action requiring the doctors to place him on a ventilator. She won the case in the High Court but the Court of Appeal set aside the order and stated that it would not order the doctors to perform any particular treatment if what the doctors were doing was in the best interests of the patient.

A contrasting situation

The facts of Baby J contrast with that of Daniel Stoneman aged 4 who has a rare brain tumour and whose mother faced possible legal action by doctors because she refuses to let him have radiotherapy. She has argued that there is only a 30% chance of success and her child has already coped with enough. To subject him to further pain and suffering is not acceptable.

At the time of writing it remains to be seen if the doctors are prepared to take the matter to court and what would be the attitude of the court. If The Baby J case is followed, then the doctors' view as to what is in the best interests of the patient may well be supported by the courts.

9

Practitioner input into this debate.

It is often the case that the nurses by their constant contact with the patient and the family can have a very detailed knowledge of the patient which the doctor does not necessarily have. It is, therefore, vital that the nurse ensures that she is able to have an input into the discussions which relate to the prognosis.

Exceptions to the lack of an enforceable right to care

In general, it is clear that patients do not have an enforceable right of action to ensure treatment and care is carried out.

There are however two areas where failure to provide a service may be actionable—not for breach of a statutory duty but rather as a result of harm occurring through negligence.

a. Emergency Services

The first is the duty of the emergency services and the accident and emergency department.

If an ambulance is called and it fails to arrive as a result of the message being lost or of some other negligence by the ambulance service and as a result of that negligence additional harm is caused to the patient, then the patient or his representative could sue in the civil courts for compensation arising from that negligence. This area is discussed in more detail in the next section. Similarly, if when a patient arrives in the accident and emergency department the patient is either not examined properly, X-Rays not taken or read properly, or an inadequate diagnosis or treatment is given, and if the patient suffers harm as a result, then a civil action might also exist. In this way the duty of care is enforced.

b. General Practitioner Services

The second area is that relating to the services of the general practitioner. The new contracts define very clearly the patients for whom the GPs are responsible, including those patients not on his list but for whom he may have responsibility in an emergency. If the GP is asked to visit a patient and fails unreasonably to attend and the patient suffers harm as a result then the patient or his representative can sue in the civil courts for negligence arising from the GP's actions or omissions. The patient has to prove negligence by the GP. It could be that the judgement made by the GP that a visit was not required was entirely appropriate in all the circumstances.

Alternatively, the patient can use the statutory complaint system and complain to the Family Health Service Authority who can set up a hearing before its medical services committee to hear the complaint. If the committee decide in favour of the complainant, it does not have the power to compensate the complainant but it does have the power to order a withholding of moneys from the GP.

It should be noticed that in both these areas the patient cannot enforce action on the part of the practitioner or service. He can only complain after the harm has been caused. If a general practitioner ceases to undertake NHS work or for some other reason asks for the patient to be removed from his list, it is the duty of the Family Health Authority to ensure that each patient has a general practitioner. In the event of no GP in the locality being prepared to take a particular patient onto his list, the FHSA has the power to require the GP to take patient for three months before the patient is transferred to another GP.

Once, however, the Accident and Emergency services or the general practitioner has provided all reasonable services and the patient is on a waiting list for either an out-patient appointment or for in-patient care, then the patient takes his chance on the resources becoming available and, as the cases already discussed have shown, has no enforceable right to health care.

Balancing Supply and Demand

The QALY Concept

Health economists have attempted to deal with the unequal ratio of demand to supply by the introduction of the concept of the QALY. This stands for 'quality-adjusted life years'. Researchers have determined the value of changes in health by asking health professionals and the general public to make an assessment of the value of changes in health. The assessments sought may be direct, e.g. asking people to rate health status on some sort of scale (like a thermometer), or indirect, through people's preference for trading off health changes against other things. Such trade-offs include the risk of death (known as 'the standard gamble') or the reduction in life expectancy (known as the 'time trade off'). QALYs have been used to illustrate where further investment could be most effective or where reduced investment would be less disruptive.

Criticisms of the Concept.

QALYs have been attacked both in relation to how they have been devised and also in relation to the whole approach.

The Oregon scheme.

An example of the difficulties and problems when attempting to put QALY thinking into practice is given by the Oregon scheme and the media publicity given to it. The scheme was based on an explicit recognition that resources available to those eligible for state care were inadequate to meet all health needs and some form of prioritising was therefore necessary. A formula was developed which would determine the priority of each of over 700 procedures on the basis of

1. How much benefit it provided.

2. How long that benefit lasted.

3. What was the cost.

A 'plimsoll line' was drawn and procedures below the line were dropped from those offered by the state on the basis that their high cost could not be justified by their very small (or very short-lived) benefits.

Inevitably, vast headlines 'SURVIVAL OF THE FITTEST' were accompanied by an article claiming that no longer was treatment to be available to anyone who needs it. Instead, health care for the poor in Oregon will depend on a computerised 714 item list of priorities decided by a mathematical formula.

Reaction in the UK

William Waldegrave, the Secretary of State in the United Kingdom at the time, said that there were no plans to introduce the Oregon project into this country. However, what would be the legality of such a determination of priorities in this country?

As we have seen, there is no absolute duty on the part of the Secretary of State to provide every possible service as part of the NHS. Section 3 of the 1977 gives considerable discretion. It could therefore be argued that for priorities to be determined in a rational way, such as that presented by the QALY concept, would be acceptable in law and would not be a breach of statutory duty.

At present it is clear that although it is accepted that not everyone can be given the treatment they need even though it is scientifically practicable, decisions over who gets what are not always made on the basis of explicit rational decision making. Demand is controlled by:

1. waiting lists for in-patients and out-patient appointments.

2. shortage of donors. (The British Kidney Patients' Association reports that since 1971, 37,000 people had died waiting for a kidney graft. About 4,000 people were on the waiting list and 2,000 had a transplant in 1990.)

3. lack of intensive treatment units/special care baby beds/coronary care places.

4. failure to staff such places even when there is a demand for them and the facilities exist.

5. shortage of expertise.

Alternative sources of help

In addition, as long as demand is not being met, some will turn to other sources of help, e.g. do-it-yourself remedies, alternative medicine, or consult pharmacists. Ann Cartwright in her review of unmet need in the 1960s concluded that there was a high proportion of patients who, for one reason or another, were not seeking health care. It is clear too that the middle classes have benefited and exploited the NHS more that the lower socio-economic groups. The failure to implement the recommendations of the Black Report is an indictment on our health care provision and it is probable that if a survey were to be undertaken now—12 years later—it would show a similar, if not worse, picture where socio-economic classes 4–6 have the worst morbidity and lowest life expectancy.

Varying local priorities

Furthermore, if we look at different conditions, certain forms of disability, ill health, or needs receive varying degrees of action across the country:

1. The availability of an abortion depends, even when the legal requirements are satisfied, not only on the facilities being available, but on the attitude of gynaecologists, some of whom interpret the Abortion Act 1967 more narrowly than others.

2. Facilities for the community care of the mentally ill and handicapped vary widely. with extreme concern being caused in some areas.

3. Treatment which might slow down the pace of AIDS is not available everywhere.

It could be argued that in the light of this irrational, uneven allocation of resources that a concept such as the QALY is preferable to the injustices which currently exist. It is clear that the additional pressures caused by the standards set by the Patients Charter will highlight the problems without necessarily producing an answer (See Chapter 8). Indeed any success is likely to be met by increased demand since the current shortages and waiting times might conceal the real demand. Patients might not be seeking help at present on the basis that there is no point, however once waiting times are reduced, such patients may come forward for treatment.

The effects of the internal market

One of the effects of the internal market will be to strengthen the determination of priorities and ensure some rational decision making. There is evidence that this is taking place. A survey carried out by the British Medical Association and published in its News Review (September 2 1992) showed that out of 20 Directors of Public Health contacted, 18 had started or were planning consultation on health care priorities. Half had said that their health authority had looked at cutting whole services including *in-vitro* fertilisation clinics or tattoo removal, and a quarter said that their health authority was considering limiting the scope of services by measures which included the imposition of age limits on patients.

However, it is always open to the Secretary of State to remind purchasers of their duty to provide a comprehensive service and not cut costs by failing to provide certain services. (see the debate on the Family Planning Services).

Reproductive Medicine

An example of the advent of new treatments bringing in its wake new demands and the assertion of new rights is the field of fertilisation and conception. The Human Fertilisation and Embryology Act 1990 attempts to answer some of the following questions in terms of the legal rights of patients:

1. *Does every one have a right to receive assistance in conception?*

   Like the other treatments discussed above, there is no absolute right for any person to receive the facilities now available from the licensed clinics within the NHS. Many are only available privately. Even for those who are prepared to pay and are medically suitable there is no absolute right. The 1990 Act and its Code of Practice places a duty upon the clinic to take into account the welfare of the future child. In one case held before the Act was passed, a patient was refused IVF because she and her husband were not deemed a suitable couple. They had been refused an adoption on the grounds of her criminal record for prostitution. The judge held that the grounds for refusing to allow her to participate in the IVF programme were reasonable. (*R. v. Ethical Advisory Committee of St. Mary's Hospital* ex parte *Harriot* 1988)

   This now has statutory endorsement.

2. *Does a single mother have the right to obtain sperm from a donor bank?*

   There is no law prohibiting the giving of sperm to a single woman but S. 13(5) requires that a licence holder treating a woman must take into account the welfare of any child who may be born as a result of treatment including the need of that child for a father.

3. *Does a woman have the right to make use of her dead husband's banked sperm?*

   This is not prohibited by the Act but the provisions of S. 13(5) would apply so there is no enforceable right but the licensed clinic would have a discretion over whether to permit its use. There is provision that the child born from the dead husband's sperm is not to be regarded in law as the child of the father. The child would therefore have no claim on his estate (S28(6)(b)). The deceased husband must have given his express consent under Schedule 3, paragraph 2(2)(b).

4. *Does a woman have control over her ejected placenta post birth?*

    This is not covered by the legislation and common law principles would apply. In the past the normal procedure has been to treat the placenta as clinical waste, but it has now been seen as having a commercial value in the pharmaceutical industry in the production of immunoglobulin. The Secretary of State gave a written answer in Parliament on 1 July 1992 that the disposal arrangements should meet with the agreement of the patients.

5. *Who owns the frozen embryos of a couple who died?*

    The Act requires that before embarking on any fertility programme, a couple should put in writing what they wish should happen to their embryos. Schedule 3 of the Act requires that it must be specified what is to happen to the eggs/sperm/embryos if the donor(s) dies.

These are only a few of the aspects which arise in relation to rights. The Act sets out a clear framework of rights and responsibilities in the law of fertilisation and embryo research. However, it does not ensure that the resources will be provided to permit those who wish to take advantage of these developments in medical technology to do so.

Questions and Exercises:

1. It is probable that there will never be the resources to meet all health needs. What priorities would you set? How do you think the equation between supply and demand could be balanced?

2. Are there minimum levels of care to which you consider patients should have a legal right? If so how would you define them?

3. The allocation of resources and the determination of priorities is part of the duty of care owed to the patient. Identify how these tasks are undertaken in your area of specialism.

4. Mrs. Walker was unsuccessful in her case. Can you envisage any circumstances where such a case should have succeeded?

5. How do you define what is meant by the best interests of the patient? Who do you think should determine what are the best interests: the patient? the relatives? the doctor? the nurse? anyone else?

Chapter 3:
The Right to Receive Reasonable Care

In contrast with the right to receive medical treatment and care, the right to receive a reasonable standard of care has a long established legal history. It derives from a recognition that compensation is payable on proof of a civil wrong (i.e. tort).

Principles of Negligence

Figure 5 sets out the elements which must be established by the person bringing an action for negligence.

Figure 5:   Negligence

Negligence in law arises when a

duty of care is broken and

causes reasonable foreseeable harm.

The test used in the Bolam case has subsequently been applied in numerous personal injury cases throughout the world to ascertain whether the medical and health professional service provided to the patient was according to the accepted standard.

The standard of care expected is:

> "the standard of the ordinary skilled man exercising and professing to have that special skill."

(McNair p.121)

The Bolam case itself was concerned with the standards of care to be given in the administration of electro-convulsive therapy. In 1954, ECT was administered without any restraint other than a mouth gag, with no relaxant drugs. The plaintiff sustained severe physical injuries consisting of the dislocation of both hip joints with fractures of the pelvis on each side. In applying the test set by the judge, the jury decided that the defendants were not negligent. Were the same facts to occur today there would, of course, be *prima facie* evidence of negligence because of improvements in the standard of care, since 1954. (*Bolam v. Friern Barnet HMC*, 1957)

The House of Lords used the Bolam Test in the case of Whitehouse and Jordan, making it clear that an error of judgement may or may not be negligence: it all depends upon the circumstances. (*Whitehouse v. Jordan*, 1981)

Different standards

In a more recent case (*Maynard v. W. Midlands RHA*, 1984), it has been accepted that different practices can be acceptable and thus the task of proving negligence has been made more difficult for the patient. In Maynard's case, a consultant physician and surgeon, whilst recognising that the most likely diagnosis of the patient's illness was T.B., took the view that Hodgkin's disease, carcinoma and sarcoidosis, were also possibilities. Because Hodgkin's disease was fatal unless remedial steps were taken in its early stages, they decided that rather than wait several weeks for the result of a sputum test, the operation of mediastinoscopy should be performed to provide a biopsy. This involved some risk of damage to the left laryngeal nerve. Unfortunately, this damage occurred but the biopsy was negative and the patient was found to have T.B. The House of Lords held that there was room for difference of opinion and practice and

> "it was not sufficient to establish negligence for the plaintiff to show that there was a body of competent professional opinion that considered the decision was wrong, if there was also a body of equally competent professional opinion that supported the decision as having been reasonable in the circumstances."

The patient therefore has to do more than find a doctor who expresses a view that the patient has been the victim of negligence. The patient has to establish that the actions, omissions or words of the doctor are such that no responsible body of medical opinion would support the doctor. If the doctor (or any other health professional defendant) is able to obtain expert evidence which justifies his actions, the judge faced by two conflicting responsible bodies of medical opinion should find against the plaintiff and in favour of the defendant.

Establishing the appropriate standards

All that has been said of the doctor is also true of the nurse, midwife and health visitor. The Bolam Test would be applied to the question as to whether there has been negligence by a practitioner. How are the standards of the appropriate nursing care determined? In practice, following an allegation that a practitioner had been negligent, the person bringing the action (the plaintiff) would have to show that the practitioner failed to follow the accepted practice and this caused the harm. The plaintiff would have to provide expert evidence of what would be regarded as accepted approved practice—possibly a leading authority in the field or a member of a professional association. This evidence could be challenged by an expert representing the practitioner. Both witnesses would give evidence in chief and be cross-examined by the other side and then re-examined on points raised in cross-examination. After the evidence has been given it is the judge who determines what was the appropriate standard which should have been followed and if there is evidence of negligence.

Standard setting

It is obviously of considerable help to the practitioner, the patient and the court if the profession has itself set standards of care. However, these will not automatically apply if there is substantial reason why in particular circumstances the facts justified an exception to the normally accepted practice. In other words, the existence of an agreed procedure does not remove from the practitioner the duty to use her professional judgement and discretion.

Implications of the Scope of Professional Practice

In a recent publication, the UKCC has suggested that the term the extended role of the practitioner is no longer appropriate; there should be a greater emphasis on the defined principles for adjusting the scope of practice rather than on certification and the emphasis on specific tasks.

The principles cover the following:

1. The interests of the client/patient.

2. Maintaining the practitioner's knowledge, skill and competence.

3. Acknowledging limits of skill etc.

4. Not jeopardising standards nor compliance with the code of Professional Conduct.

5. Recognising direct and personal accountability.

6. Avoiding inappropriate delegation.

If the practitioner acts in areas where she lacks the skill, knowledge or competence and harm occurs to the patient, then the practitioner will be professionally liable and the employer may be vicariously liable for her negligence. The courts are not concerned as to whether a doctor or nurse carries out a particular activity except where there is a statutory provision regulating the position. The court is concerned that the patient receives the appropriate standard of care. It is no defence to a court action of negligence to say that the defendant had not been qualified for long or was a nurse and not a doctor. The patient is entitled to receive the appropriate standard of care and this should be provided by the necessary supervision of those who have less experience.

One of the values of the UKCC paper on the scope of professional practice is that it firmly places responsibility upon the individual practitioner to ensure that she is competent before she undertakes any activity and this is more important than traditional lines of demarcation between nurse and doctor.

Protection of the practitioner

The practitioner is entitled to protection against allegations of negligence, where he has acted appropriately in all the circumstances, but this may mean a patient receives no compensation for harm.

This is because at the heart of our present system of compensation for medical accidents is proof of 'fault'. There must be established culpability by the defendant who has been found to fail the Bolam Test.

'The thing speaks for itself'

The patient or plaintiff has the best chance of succeeding if he can establish a *res ipsa loquitur* situation—the thing speaks for itself:

- amputating the left rather than the right leg;
- operating on the wrong patient;
- leaving a swab in the operation site without being aware of it;
- giving insufficient oxygen or the appropriate gases during an operation.

Such circumstances will result in the defendant being called on to establish that there was no negligence on his part. More likely, such circumstances may lead to an offer of compensation being made and the dispute will therefore be concentrated on issues relating to quantum—how much compensation—rather than liability itself.

Causation

Proving fault is only the first hurdle for the seeker of compensation. One of the greatest difficulties is establishing causation—since the law of the tort of negligence requires the plaintiff to establish that it was the breach of duty, i.e. the negligent act or omission which caused the harm suffered by the plaintiff.

Many recent cases illustrate the difficulty of plaintiffs satisfying this requirement of proving causation.

1. The House of Lords held that it had not been established that an admitted excess of oxygen (caused when the catheter to measure levels was inserted into a vein rather than an artery) had caused the retrolental fibroplasia suffered by the premature baby and ordered the case to go for retrial. (*Wilsher v. Essex AHA*, 1986)

2. The mother of a brain-damaged baby had not established the causal connection of the whooping cough vaccination to claim compensation. (*Loveday v. Renton et al.*, 1988)

3. In a well-publicised case, parents of a boy who was given a large overdose of penicillin in treatment for his meningitis had not satisfactorily established that it was the overdose of penicillin rather than the meningitis that caused the deafness and so were unable to obtain compensation for the deafness. (*Kay v. Ayrshire & Arran Health Board*, 1987)

Medical science is at an early stage in terms of our understanding of what causes what. We have little idea of how ECT or the various neuroleptic drugs work. To establish that *B* was reasonably foreseeably caused by *A* is often an impossible hurdle for the plaintiff to surmount. However, this is what our present laws of causation require the plaintiff to do.

Evidence in court

The plaintiff has the burden of proof, and in civil cases this must be established on a balance of probabilities. Evidence has to be secured by witnesses, through contemporaneous records, and by experts, that a breach of the duty of care, which has caused reasonably foreseeable harm, has occurred. There is no clear duty on professional staff to notify the patient if an untoward incident has occurred, whether or not it is the result of negligence, and the patient may often be dependent upon the altruism of the professional or signs and symptoms which are out of the ordinary. In the earlier cases on disclosure of medical information, the courts spoke strongly against the possibility of patients seeking access to records in order to initiate 'fishing expeditions'. Access was only permitted if there were already in existence *prima facie* evidence that a claim existed.

This situation has changed as we shall see when we look at rights of access to records, but the patient still has to have a modicum of suspicion and a certain amount of knowledge to launch an investigation, unless there is recognised in law a positive duty to warn the patient that compensatable harm has occurred. I remember a Scottish doctor boasting at an International Conference that his worst blunder led to an unsuspecting widower thanking him for the care he had given his wife, who had unfortunately died, and presenting him with a bottle of whisky, whereas a patient over whom he lavished his whole-hearted care and skill threatened to sue him.

Difficulties in getting evidence

A recent Court of Appeal case shows the difficulty for the plaintiff in getting evidence and proving causation. The plaintiff, Mrs. Sellers, was admitted to the Royal Victoria Hospital, Bournemouth with a threatened miscarriage. She was cared for by a consultant registrar and houseman.

Figure 6a: Hurdles for Plaintiff

a.	Elements of Negligence	—	Duty Breach Causation Harm
b.	Burden of Proof	—	Balance of Probabilities
c.	Costs		
d.	Gambling against a payment in.		

Figure 6b: Court Proceedings

Plaintiff calls witnesses in turn:

    a.   Examination-in-chief
    b.   Cross Examination
    c.   Re-examination

Judge could find for defendant at this point

Defendant calls witnesses in turn:

    a.   Examination-in-chief
    b.   Cross Examination
    c.   Re-examination

The Consultant diagnosed an inevitable abortion and ordered drug treatment to be stopped and if there were no miscarriage as a matter of course it should be assisted by drip. The plaintiff subsequently had a miscarriage in unpleasant circumstances. Amongst other issues, she alleged the drug regime in the drip was wrong. The trial judge awarded her £2,500 damages holding that the registrar who was abroad at the time of the trial was the 'real culprit' for the composition of the drip. When Mrs. Sellers wished to use the registrar on his return from abroad as a witness to prove that the original diagnosis of a threatened abortion was incorrect, she was refused permission on various grounds, including the fact that she had failed to prove that had it not been for the abortion, the foetus would have survived to ordinary maturity. (*Sellers v. Cooke, et al.* 1990). There are considerable difficulties faced by a person bringing an action for negligence and some of these are listed in figure 6a.

Financing a court action

Even if the plaintiff would appear to have a *prima facie* case with evidence of witnesses and records and experts, the financial risks and costs in commencing action are formidable. Rules controlling those entitled to support from Legal Aid funds have considerably reduced the number of those eligible. Most potential plaintiffs receive too much income to receive legal aid, but too little to finance themselves with peace of mind.

Should the plaintiff lose, then the usual rule is that costs of both parties are paid by the unsuccessful party. Only a few days in the High Court can result in thousands of pounds of costs. The libel action involving Esther Rantzen of '*That's Life*' led to £150,000 being paid as compensation to the plastic surgeon who was defamed, but the BBC had to meet costs of over £1 million.

Payment into court

The gambling nature of litigation is highlighted by the dilemmas faced by a plaintiff if the defendant makes a payment into court. If the plaintiff refuses the payment in, and the judge eventually awards less than that payment, then the plaintiff pays the costs of both sides, which can easily exceed the level of compensation awarded by the judge. On the other hand, if the plaintiff refuses the payment in and the judge awards more than that, then the plaintiff receives the larger sum and the defendant pays the costs of both plaintiff and defence. A carefully fixed payment in can put a plaintiff in a very delicate situation, particularly in a case where liability has not been admitted and is still to be established, or where precedents on quantum are few and weak.

Nor is our legal system designed to facilitate the progress of cases, though recent major changes to the jurisdiction of the different courts may assist the parties. For example, cases of up to £50,000 must now be taken in the County Court instead of the High Court where the previous limit was £5,000. There are doubts as to whether our dual system of solicitors and barristers is an advantage to the parties and certainly the possibility that the barrister who has advised a party throughout the case and drafted the pleadings, may not in fact be the lawyer representing that party at the trial, is a real one.

Recent improvements

One improvement in recent years to the chance of the plaintiff succeeding has been the change to the rules relating to time limits. Cases of personal injury and death had to be brought within three years from the time of action accruing—i.e. three years from the date of the incident which caused the harm.

The injustice of this could be seen in those cases where the plaintiff might not even know within the three years that he was suffering harm in such

Figure 7: Improvements to Plaintiff's Chances

1.	Time Limits
2.	Multi-Party Actions
3.	Compensation without proof of fault — Vaccine Damage Payment Act
4.	Procedural Changes in Civil Cases

cases as pneumoconiosis or asbestosis. The law was therefore changed so that time did not run against the plaintiff until he had knowledge that the injury was significant, attributable to negligence, and the identity of the defendant. Knowledge includes facts which he could reasonably have been expected to acquire.

In addition, the judge has a general discretion in personal injury cases to extend the time limits where it would be equitable to allow an action to proceed having regard to the degree to which the time limits would prejudice the plaintiff. He must however take into account whether the defendant would be prejudiced by waiving the time limits.

Persons under an incapacity

Furthermore, it has for long been the rule that where the plaintiff is under an incapacity—e.g. such as being a minor or being mentally ill, then time does not run until the incapacity is removed. This can mean that a case first comes before court many years after the incident allegedly causing the harm took place. Thus, in one case, a mother obtained damages for negligence during the confinement 17 years after the birth of her twins. (*Bull v. Wakeham*, 1989)

Multi-party actions

An interesting recent development is multi-party actions where many patients who claim to have suffered from the same cause, especially drugs, combine together in one action. Courts have slowly devised rules of accepting such actions and potential plaintiffs may benefit.

Other ways of obtaining compensation

What about other ways of obtaining compensation without going through the merry go round of the legal system?

Schemes of statutory compensation

There is an increasing number of statutes which allow compensation without proof of fault. For example, the Vaccine Damages Payment Act 1979 makes available a sum of £20,000 as compensation for individuals who have suffered serious disability following vaccinations without proving that any one is at fault. In a sense, it is society's payment to those victims who suffer in order that the rest may be effectively protected from various infectious diseases. Even though the payment has increased from £10,000 to £20,000, it is woefully inadequate for seriously brain-damaged victims in comparison with the financial consequences of such a condition, and indeed in comparison with the present levels of compensation available if fault can be proved and payment ordered through the civil courts.

Criminal injury compensation

Another form of compensation is through our criminal injury compensation system, but here it would be necessary to prove that a crime had been committed, for example, a criminal act of attempted murder or gross negligence, and then compensation is payable. The ultimate payment is closer to that paid under the tort system of compensation than under the current statutory compensation schemes. The proportion of persons who receive compensation for medical accidents or crimes under these alternative schemes is, however, a minute proportion of the total number.

Failures in bringing legal action

It is not surprising from a review of the hurdles in the tort system and the lack of alternative, effective systems that a high proportion of potential litigants give up early on or ultimately fail to obtain compensation.

Figures provided by the Department of Health for 1990/91 showed that £45 million was spent by the NHS in meeting claims for medical negligence. In 35 cases, damages exceeded £300,000 each—amounting to about £17 million. The remaining £28 million covered about 7,000 cases where the average per case was about £6,500. The same paper reports that about 95% of medical negligence cases are settled out of court.

An indicator of the increase in litigation is the increase in number of clients contacting the Action for Victims of Medical Accidents (AVMA), a registered charity. In its annual report for 1989 it reports a case load of 5,500 which is a growth of 4,500 since September 1988.

The Pearson Report

A Royal Commission (The Pearson) was set up to investigate civil liability and compensation for personal injuries. It reported in 1978 and concluded that

"We considered the possibility of abolishing tort for two other categories of injury, medical and ante-natal. In relation to medical injuries, it was put to us that it was particularly difficult to prove negligence and still more important, that it was often impossible to ascertain whether or not the injury was indeed a medical injury. It might not be clear whether a given deterioration in the patient's condition would have occurred but for the act or omission complained of. It was also put to us that there were widespread fears that the risk of litigation was proving an obstacle to good and economical medical practice, and that, if litigation became more common, insurance premiums might rise to prohibitive levels. But we did not find these arguments strong enough to justify making medical injuries a special case where tort liability would not apply, especially as we received much evidence from medical and other witnesses which favoured the retention of tort."

Very little has changed in our system for compensation since the Pearson report was published. Demands for a radical revision continue to be made. Some have called for the introduction of a No-Fault Scheme such as operates in New Zealand, Finland and Sweden. Basically the system provides for those who become victims of medical misfortune to receive compensation without proving someone was at fault. The compensation is funded in a variety of ways usually a mixture of government and insurance-based schemes.

One critic of our present tort system, Donald Harris, Director of the Oxford Centre for Socio-Legal Studies, stated at an AVMA annual conference that no improvement in patient care has been achieved by the tort system and cited research in New York carried out by the Harvard Law School that doctors did not alter their procedures in response to specific medical negligence cases. An analysis of the medical records of 31,000 patients discharged from 51 hospitals showed that only 1 in 8 of those who were victims of negligence brought a claim for damages and of these only half succeeded in their claim, the average time between injury and payment being 6 years.

Alternative Dispute resolution

In the face of the obvious inefficiencies of our present system for obtaining compensation the Lord Chancellor has recommended a switch to an alternative dispute resolution.

The Consultation document issued by the Department of Health sets out possible arrangements based on Lord Griffiths's proposals for the introduction of a system of arbitration in the NHS. The proposal is for a panel of three, comprising two doctors nominated one by each party and a lawyer skilled in medical negligence work and agreed to by both parties to provide arbitration within the general framework of the Arbitration Acts. Oral evidence would not normally be taken. However, the scheme retains the element of fault and the Bolam Test would be used as the test of negligence. The scheme assumes that there would be no appeal to the courts other than on points of law.

Comments on the proposals are currently being invited on its feasibility, desirability and value.

The danger if such a system is set up alongside the court system is that it could become yet another hurdle for potential claimants to surmount in determining how to set about claiming compensation, speedily and effectively.

Extending the powers of the Health Service Commissioner

An alternative system apart from the introduction of a no-fault system may be to give greater powers to the health service commissioner. At present his jurisdiction to handle complaints does not include aspects of clinical judgement and if he envisages that the ultimate aim of the complainant is to obtain compensation he is hesitant to investigate the complaint.

He has no direct power to order health authorities to make financial payments to complainants, but he can recommend that such payments are made and his recommendations and reports are submitted to the House of Commons Select Committee which has the power to make further investigations and question health authority officers and members who have shown a deliberate disregard for the recommendations of the Ombudsman. The proposal to widen the HSC's jurisdiction to include complaints relating to clinical judgement has been criticised on the grounds that it would subject health professionals to a double jeopardy. The complainant could use the HSC to carry out the preliminary investigation and then use the resulting evidence to mount a civil claim. Such critics demand the protection of ensuring that before such an HSC investigation took place, the complainant should sign away any legal rights to pursue the action in the courts of law. At present, such an agreement is not legally enforceable and even if such provision could be set up it might be questioned as to whether it is ethical to prevent a person, who did not appreciate that there were grounds for seeking compensation in the civil courts, from seeking a legal remedy.

Need for reform

However, it is clear that major reforms are essential not only to facilitate the recovery of compensation by the injured person, but also to assist the health service body faced with meeting potentially crippling claims. Health Authorities have assumed the duty to indemnify injured patients and have thus taken away the burden on Medical Defence Bodies in respect of NHS claims against doctors and dentists. Even though structured settlements might reduce the impact of a large claim, the smaller NHS Trusts may still find that the burden of meeting large claims will lead to a reduction of their current revenue moneys.

Reform is therefore urgently required.

The NHS Trusts and the internal market

How far does the existence of NHS Trusts affect the situation?

Clearly the agreement drawn up between provider and purchaser will include quality standards expected in the delivery of services. Negligence by the professional staff employed by the Trust could therefore not only give rise to an action for vicariously liability of the Trust because it employed the staff who were negligent in course of employment, it could also give rise to sanctions being applied by the purchaser because the Trust was in breach of the standards set in the agreement. However, this action will not take place in a court of law since section 4 of the National Health Service and Community Care Act 1990 prevents this occurring. If an agreement between provider and purchaser over the issue cannot be reached, then the Secretary of State can appoint an adjudicator to determine the issue.

It is also conceivable that if the purchaser has in some way failed in setting standards or making provision, that the health service body acting as purchaser also could be the subject of litigation, as well as the provider. This possibility still has to be seen.

Implications for the nurse, midwife and health visitor

It is clear that the inclusion of the fault element as the basis of the payment of compensation will continue for the immediate future. Crucial to the issue of liability will therefore be the question of what standards were followed and which should have been followed. The practitioner should therefore follow the guidelines set out below:

1. Inform herself of the guidelines for any given situation.

2. Monitor the extent to which these are followed.

3. Follow the advice of the UKCC in its Code of Professional Conduct.

4. If conflicts exist between the Code and the Instructions of Management, ensure that these are taken up, preferably in writing, with senior management.

5. Ensure that training is maintained to develop skills knowledge and competence in the light of rising standards.

27

Questions and Exercises

1. Use the Bolam Test to identify what would be the approved practice in any given procedure. What difficulties do you encounter in applying the test?

2. Are you aware of differences in practice and procedure? How would these affect the patients claim for compensation should harm occur?

3. Try to apply the principle of the Bolam Test to the non-clinical areas of patient care. What difficulties arise from this?

4. Consider the advantages and disadvantages which arise from a system of no-fault liability. Which system is best from the patient's point of view? Which system is best from the professional's point of view?

Chapter 4:
Consent to Treatment

Trespass to the person

One of the most ancient of our legal actions is that of trespass —any direct interference with land, goods or the person is actionable without the need to prove any damage : the mere touching is sufficient to constitute grounds for legal action. A trespass to the person constitutes a battery.

Consent as a defence to an action for trespass to the person

The willing consent of a competent person is a complete defence to an action for trespass to the person.

Evidence that treatment has been undertaken without the patient's consent will enable a patient to seek compensation, even though the patient has benefited from the treatment, unless specific exceptional circumstances exist.

Still a trespass even if for the benefit of an individual.

It would have come as a surprise to the surgeon who, during an abdominal operation, noticed that the patient had an ingrowing toe nail and altruistically sorted it out, to be faced with a claim for compensation to the person. Yet his Defence Union made a payment without disputing liability. No exceptional circumstances applied and the patient had not consented to this interference to his person.

No particular form of consent required

There is no legal requirement that consent should be given in writing. Consent by word of mouth or even by implication—i.e. by non-verbal behaviour can be valid. Clearly, however, if there is a dispute, then written evidence is of far greater weight.

Furthermore, if a patient has signed a consent form, it is very difficult for the patient in the absence of fraud or compulsion to maintain an action for trespass to the person. In spite of evidence from nursing staff that patients often do not know what they are signing for, the mere fact of the signature on the form would prevent an action for trespass to the person succeeding.

This was the dicta in *Chatterton v Gerson* (1981). In this case, Miss Chatterton suffered chronic and intractable pain following a hernia operation. She was treated by the defendant, a specialist in the treatment of chronic intractable pain. She received two spinal injections. The second caused complete numbness of her leg and considerably impaired her mobility. She claimed that she had not been warned of this risk and therefore had not consented to the operation.

The Judge held that once the patient had been informed in broad terms of the intended treatment and had given consent, the patient could not then say there had been a lack of real consent.

If there is an absence of consent and no exceptional circumstances exist, then a trespass to the person action is a powerful remedy in law. Proof of harm does not have to be established; the trespass is sufficient in itself to constitute a wrong.

The Patient's autonomy

A recent tragic case saw the death of a mother who had just given birth to twins and had refused a blood transfusion because she was a Jehovah's Witness. It was stated afterwards that there was no certainty that a blood transfusion would have saved her life. However, that chance was not taken. Her autonomy and her belief that there are values more important than life itself were respected.

This principle of autonomy was recently stressed by the Court of Appeal in a case Re T involving the 20 year-old daughter whose mother was Jehovah's Witness. She refused to have life-saving blood transfusion and the case was brought to court by the doctors and by the father. The Court of Appeal emphasised that the doctors in considering whether to accept an adult patient's refusal to consent to treatment which in their clinical judgement was necessary, should consider whether the patient's decision had been intended to apply to the particular circumstances or whether the capacity to decide had been affected by shock, pain, drugs or overbearing outside influence. The court supported the view that the daughter's mind had been unduly influenced by the mother and the court ordered the treatment to proceed.

A further weakening of the patient's autonomy is seen in a recent case. This authorised treatment to proceed against wishes of a mentally competent adult, capable of making that decision. The case, reported in the press on 14 October 1992, authorised a caesarian section to be performed upon a mother who had refused treatment on religious grounds. The mother, who had two children, was admitted to hospital with labour complications. Her baby's birth had been predicted for October 6th. Doctors did their best to persuade the woman that the only means of saving her life and that of her child was to carry out a caesarian section. The woman, supported by her husband, had refused to submit herself to the operation because of her religious beliefs. The court was contacted at 1.25 pm, and the hearing started at 1.55. The decision was made at 2.18 pm by Sir Stephen Brown, President of the High Court Family Division, who agreed that the declaration could be made which authorised the operation to take place. Sir Stephen accepted the doctors' that the baby could not be born alive if the caesarian section was not carried out and that the situation was desperate. Unfortunately, the baby died but the mother survived, though in a serious condition. The full judgement is awaited. Its implications for midwives are many, since this is the first time that the court has overruled the wishes of the mother in order to save the life of the unborn child. The question now is to what extent could this principle be followed in other areas such as diet, smoking, home/hospital confinement etc?

Unconscious patient with card

There is no UK equivalent of a recent Canadian case and it is difficult to predict what would have been the outcome in this country. In *Malette v. Shulman* (1991), the patient aged 57 was seriously injured in a road accident and admitted unconscious to hospital. The defendant's doctor diagnosed incipient shock from loss of blood. He ordered intravenous glucose followed by Ringer's Lactate. A Jehovah's Witness card, found in the plaintiff's purse requested that no blood be administered 'under any circumstances'. The doctor although aware of the card, personally administered blood transfusions he considered necessary to preserve the patient's life. The patient survived and sued the doctor. The trial judge awarded c$20,000 (Canadian dollars) to the patient, holding that the card was a valid restriction of the doctor's right to treat the plaintiff which he was not entitled to ignore. The doctor appealed to the Ontario Court of Appeal and lost his appeal—the card imposed a valid restriction, even though the patient was unconscious, since the card was intended to cover the situation where advice was not possible. In addition, the State's interest in protecting the lives and health of its citizens and the integrity of the medical profession did not prevent a competent adult from refusing life-preserving medical treatment.

The card read as in figure 8.

Figure 8:   No Blood Transfusions

As one of Jehovah's Witnesses with firm religious convictions, I request that no blood or blood products be administered to me under any circumstances. I fully realise the implications of this position, but I have resolutely decided to obey the Bible command:

'Keep abstaining .... from blood'.

(Acts 15 : 28, 29)

However, I have no religious objection to use the non blood alternatives, such as Dextran, Haemaccel, PVP, Ringer's Lactate or saline solution.

(translation of the original French)

In this country, it is clear from the ruling in the Court of Appeal discussed above that the doctors would have a clear duty to examine the validity of this written refusal in the light of the particular circumstances of the present situation, and if they had any reason to question whether the statement purported to be the true views of the patient, to give life-saving treatment. They could always have recourse to the view of the Courts (as happened in Re T) but time might prevent this as a realistic possibility.

A right to die?

In Re T, the Court emphasised that what was under discussion was not the right to die, but the right of a patient to live as he/she wished and choose the treatment, and the Court emphasised that this right existed. In certain circumstances, therefore, the patient is entitled to refuse treatment even if it is life saving.

The right to commit suicide

Since 1961 it has not been a crime to commit suicide. Any person, therefore, who takes an action to end his/her life and fails cannot then be prosecuted for attempting to commit suicide.

Illegality of aiding and abetting a suicide

However any person who aids and abets another to attempt to or to commit suicide is guilty of an offence. The practitioner can therefore under no circumstances assist a patient to end his/her life. To do so is a crime.

Euthanasia, the facilitation of those who wish to die, is not recognised in the law of this country. The recent prosecution of Consultant Nigel Cox following his administration of potassium chloride to a dying patient shows the difficulties for the practitioner in this area. Drugs can be given to relieve pain even if they incidentally have the side effect of shortening life, provided that is not the intention. Drugs cannot be given to shorten life, even if they incidentally relieve pain. The prosecution has the burden of establishing that the defendant intended to cause death or was grossly negligent as to whether death would occur as a result of his actions. (1992)

Other defences to an action for trespass

What are the exceptional circumstances which would enable treatment to be given without consent without giving rise to a trespass to the person?

The common law power to act out of necessity

The first is the right to act out of necessity in the best interests of another. This defence was used successfully in a case involving suffragettes who went on a hunger strike whilst in prison. They were force-fed and on their release sued for trespass to the person, but lost the case. The judge held

"It was the duty both under the rules, and apart from the rules, of the officials to preserve the health and lives of the prisoners who were in the custody of the Crown. If they forcibly fed the plaintiff when it was not necessary, the defendants ought to pay damages."

The jury after considering for two minutes, returned a verdict for the defendants.

The right to act out of necessity has been conventionally described as the common law power of the professional and has been used to justify a wide range of action where there are no statutory provisions. The House of Lords had the task of defining what was meant by this power in a case involving the sterilisation of a mentally handicapped woman aged 35 years. (*ReF*. 1989)

Their conclusion was that in a case where the patient was incapable of giving consent, a doctor who acted out of necessity in the best interests of the patient and followed the accepted approved professional practice according to the Bolam Test was acting lawfully. Necessity included not just life-saving action but day-to-day care which was essential for the patient's well being. There are many who question the placing of the decision making on behalf of the mentally incapacitated patient entirely upon the shoulders of the professional, except for reference to the court in situations of non-therapeutic sterilisation, but at present there is a vacuum in law—neither relatives, nor guardians, nor proxy decision makers have the legal right to give consent in relation to health care.

The Law Commission has recently produced a consultancy paper on 'Mentally Incapacitated Adults—Decision making', exploring the problems and potential solutions and legislation may eventually be proposed.

Powers under the Mental Health Act 1983

Other exceptional circumstances which might justify action which would otherwise be a trespass to the person include Part IV of the Mental Health Act 1983 which enables treatment to be given without the consent of the detained patient in carefully defined circumstances and according to specific conditions. The giving of treatment in these situations is monitored by the Mental Health Act Commission, which has a statutory duty to act on behalf of the Secretary of State in the review of the exercise of powers and discharge of duties under the Act, visiting and interviewing, and hearing complaints from detained patients.

Force feeding in prisons is now governed by regulations and apart from Public Health statutes there are no other circumstances where treatment can be given compulsorily by Act of Parliament.

Consent in particular circumstances

1. Minors

Minors of 16 and 17 years have a statutory right to give consent to treatment which includes diagnostic procedures as well as anaesthetics for medical and dental treatment. This consent does not prevent the parents also giving consent for the 16 and 17 year old but in the event of a clash between parent and child it would be unreasonable in most circumstances for the professional to take the parental consent and inflict treatment on an unwilling minor of this age.

This issue arose in the case of a 16-year old girl who suffered from anorexia nervosa (Re J 1992). At the date of the hearing, she had refused to eat for nine days, had lost 8 lbs in 14 days and weighed 5 st.7 lb although 5 ft. 7 in. tall. The court decided that it had a duty to override her wishes. The court had power under its *parens patriae* jurisdiction even when the minor was competent (under the Gillick ruling) to make a decision which overruled the minor.

It is interesting that the court made no reference to Mental Health legislation. Sometimes patients with anorexia nervosa are placed under compulsory sections of the Mental Health Act so that treatment can be given under Part IV provisions. The Court of Appeal relied upon the fact that the girl was only 16 and therefore came under the inherent jurisdiction of the court to care for minors.

Minors under 16 years

For minors below the age of 16 years, parents have the power to consent. However, if they refuse to give consent in circumstances where the child's life is at risk the professional would have the right to act in the best interests of the child and, in an emergency situation, would not have to wait for an order of the court. In addition, the Gillick case established that where the minor had sufficient maturity to understand the nature of the proposed treatment and the capacity to make a decision in her own right, then parental consent did not have to be obtained. The court was concerned with the issue over family planning, but its statement of principle could apply to other fields of health care.

The Children Act 1989

The underlying philosophy of this Act is that the views of the child should where possible be taken into account. So for example Section 38(6) states in relation to the making of interim orders:

Where the court makes an interim care order, or interim supervision order, it may give such directions (if any) as it considers appropriate with regard to the medical or psychiatric examination or other assessment of the child; *but if the child is of sufficient understanding to make an informed decision he may refuse to submit to the examination or other assessment.*

Similar words to those italicised are also included in the Act in relation to child assessment orders (S.43(8)); emergency protection orders (44(7)) and psychiatric and medical examination and treatment (Schedule 3 paragraphs 4 and 5).

In the Re J case discussed above, the Court of Appeal held that its decision to overrule the wishes of the minor suffering from anorexia nervosa were consistent with the duty of the court to make the child's welfare the paramount consideration and was not inconsistent with the sections and schedules cited above.

Research on a minor

There is a doubtful legal situation where consent for research upon a minor is required. There is justification for saying that a parent cannot give a valid consent to research procedures which are not in the best interests of the child or where there is a significant risk. Where the child is likely to benefit from the therapeutic aspects of the research different considerations apply. Where the child will not receive any personal benefit from the research, there can be no justification in submitting the child to even minor risk.

Consent has sometimes been given by parents for one child to be a donor for another child, for example in the donation of bone marrow. However, in cases where there is doubt as to whether such donation is in the best interests of the donor child, the views of the court could be sought.

2. Mentally disordered

Where an adult lacks the mental capacity to make a decision on a particular issue in relation to her care and treatment on the authority of Re F, the professional should act in the best interests of the patient. Practitioners are sometimes asked to give written consent on behalf of a patient who is incapable of giving consent.

For example, a person with learning disabilities may require dental treatment and the dentist might ask a practitioner to sign the form on behalf of the patient consenting to the treatment. The practitioner does not at present have the right in law to give such consent. Nor does the relative of the patient. If treatment is considered by the dentist to be in the best interest of the patient, then he should proceed with it. An appropriate form for such purposes can be found in the NHS executive's booklet on consent to treatment and is produced in figure 9.

3. Husband and Wife or Cohabitee

The law gives no authority to either a spouse or cohabitee to give consent on behalf of the partner, even when the patient is unconscious or requiring

Figure 9:   Consent form

Medical or dental treatment of a patient who is unable to consent because of mental disorder

Health Authority . . . .
Hospital . . . .
Unit Number . . . .

Patient's Surname . . . .
Other Names . . . .
Date of Birth . . . .
Sex: (please tick)   Male ☐ Female ☐

NOTE

If there is any doubt the ability of a mentally disordered patient to give consent to treatment, the Registered Medical Practitioner in charge of the patient should be asked to interview the patient. If, in his or her opinion, the patient is able to give valid consent to medical, dental or surgical treatment, he or she should be asked to do so and no-one further should be involved.

If the patient is considered unable to give valid consent it this considered good practice to discuss any proposed treatment with the next of kin.

For surgical or dental operations the form should also be signed by the Registered Medical or Dental Practitioner who carries out the treatment.

Doctors/Dentists

Describe investigation,operation or treatment involved

Complete this part of the form

In my opinion . . . . is not capable of giving consent to treatment.
In my opinion the treatment proposed is in his/her best interests and should be given.

The patient's next of kin have/have not been informed. *(delete as necessary)*

Date: . . . .

Signature

. . . .

Name of Registered Medical Practitioner in charge of the patient

. . . .

Signature

. . . .

Name of Second Registered Medical/Dental Practitioner who is providing treatment

. . . .

an operation for sterilisation. It would be good professional practice to get the views of the partner where this is appropriate but the partner does not have any right of veto.

Information-giving and negligence

In *Chatterton v. Gerson* it was held that if the patient had signed the consent form, then in the absence of fraud or compulsion, an action for trespass to the person could not succeed. Where the patient was alleging that she did not have sufficient information to appreciate the risks involved in undergoing the treatment and she suffered harm, then the appropriate action was one in negligence not in trespass.

The negligence action was based on the principle that the doctor's duty of care to the patient included the duty to inform the patient of the risks and implications of the proposed treatment. If he were in breach of this duty and the patient suffered harm then the patient might have a successful claim against the doctor. But how much information is the patient entitled to have? When could negligence be established?

This was the issue before the House of Lords in the Sidaway case (*Sidaway v. Bethlehem Royal Hospital Governors*, 1985). The facts were Mrs. Amy Sidaway suffered from persistent pain in her neck and shoulders and was advised to have an operation. The surgeon warned her of the possibility of disturbing a nerve root but did not mention the possibility of damage to the spinal chord, which was less than 1%. She consented to the operation, but the spinal column was damaged and she was left severely disabled.

The speeches in the House of Lords, with the exception of Lord Scarman, showed a reluctance to take the American road and the doctrine of 'informed consent' accepted in the States was denied any place in our jurisdiction. Instead the majority applied the Bolam Test to the duty of giving information to a patient.

> "The merit of the Bolam Test is that the criterion of the duty of care owed by a doctor to his patient is whether he has acted in accordance with a practice accepted as proper by a body of responsible and skilled medical opinion."

Diplock p.657

What are the patients' rights then?

The right consists of being given information about significant risks of substantial harm.

> "To decide what risks the existence of which a patient should be voluntarily warned and the terms in which such warning, if any, should be given, having regard to

the effect that warning may have, is as much an exercise of professional skill and judgement as any other part of the doctor's comprehensive duty of care to the individual patient."

Diplock p.659.

Therapeutic privilege

Do all patients have to be given this information?

The answer is No. The Courts recognised the existence of the right of therapeutic privilege.

"An obligation to give a patient all the information available to the doctor would often be inconsistent with the Doctor's contractual obligation to have regard to the patient's best interests. Some information might confuse, other information might alarm a particular patient, ... the doctor must decide in the light of his training and experience and in the light of his knowledge of the patient what should be said and how it should be said"

Lord Templeman p.665.

The principles of the Bolam Test would be applied to defining the standard of care to be followed in both the giving of and withholding information from the patient.

A similar principle has been used in the statutes relating to access to information as we shall see in Chapter 5. There is no absolute right for a patient to receive all the relevant information. A paternalistic attitude is clearly apparent in judicial and parliamentary thinking on this issue.

Nor is it easy for a plaintiff to succeed in this type of action. The courts insist on the plaintiff establishing that had he known of the significant risks of substantial harm (of which the doctor failed to inform him), then he would not have had that operation or treatment. It is very difficult to prove you would have done X, if you had known of Y, instead of Z if the possibility of Y had never occurred to you. This has undoubtedly been a major obstacle to claims for compensation succeeding.

In one case, a patient was able to obtain compensation even though it was accepted that she would still have gone ahead with the treatment had she known of the risks. In this case, an unsuccessful repeat operation to drain a cyst on the cervical spine of a young woman caused immediate tetraplegia. The doctor decided not to warn her that there was a substantial risk of total paralysis of up to 25% from the operation even when competently done and that on the other hand, total paralysis would supervene in nine months if the condition remained untreated. The patient was awarded £3,000 for shock and depression consequent upon discovering without prior warning that she had been rendered tetraplegic. (1991)

The difficulties of succeeding in this kind of action can be seen from the case of *Blyth v. Bloomsbury Health Authority* 1987 where the plaintiff complained that she had been given insufficient information about the contraceptive drug Depo-Provera which caused unpleasant side effects. The Court of Appeal applied the Sidaway principle and held that:

> "the amount of information to be given must depend upon the circumstances and as a general proposition it is governed by what is called the 'Bolam Test'. Information that the Hospital doctor possesses as a result of her own research did not have to be passed on to the patient."

Clearly, however, if a case succeeds, there is the likelihood of improvements in communication. This happened in the field of sterilisation. In the case of *Thake v. Maurice*, the plaintiffs, a married couple, did not wish to have any more children and the husband underwent a vasectomy in October 1975. In 1977 the wife became pregnant again. They won their case against the defendant on the ground that he failed to give his usual warning that there was a slight risk that the husband could become fertile again. Compensation of £11,177 was awarded. (1984)

Warnings about the possibility of the treatment not being completely successful.

It is now standard practice to warn patients that there is a risk that the sterilisation might not succeed and cannot be 100% guaranteed with the usual surgery.

The NHS Management Executive has recently published guidance on consent for examination and treatment and this includes a specimen form for the patient and professional to sign. Separate forms are available for health professionals other than doctors or dentists and there is also a form for a doctor or dentist to sign in the case of a patient unable to consent because of mental disorder (see figure 9). This would be based on the principles set out by the House of Lords in Re F and cover mentally disordered patients who do not come under the provisions of Part IV of the Mental Health Act 1983. The form does not cover the situation where the patient refuses to consent because of mental disorder.

The guidance given in this booklet has been criticised as a wrong interpretation of the House of Lords decision in Sidaway. It is clear that it would be an advantage to both practitioners and to patients if there were clear statutory provisions establishing the nature of the patient's rights to receive appropriate, relevant information before deciding whether to take a particular course of treatment.

Guidelines for the practitioner

1. Has the competence of the patient/client/resident to make a particular decision been determined?.

2. What information should reasonably be given to the patient/client/ resident to assist him/her in making the decision?

3. If the person lacks the competence to make the decision, who should be involved in advising on the appropriate course of action?

4. Does the professional have the power to act without the consent of the person?

5. If so define what is the source of this power.

6. Should the courts be involved?

Exceptions to the Sidaway principle:

Whilst in general there is not an absolute duty to disclose to the patient every piece of relevant information in order to obtain a valid consent, in certain cases it could be said that the circumstances justify giving full information to the patient.

Information given to participants in Research

It is suggested that where the patient is participating in a research programme then more should be disclosed to the participant of the risks involved especially where the research has no therapeutic benefit for the participant (Brazier p. 418). Whilst this duty is laid down in the Helsinki Declaration on the code of ethics on research on humans and in the Department of Health circulars, it has not yet come before the courts. The argument would be that if the full information relating to risks and side effects is not given to the participant, then their consent in the research programme has been obtained by deception. If there is no therapeutic benefit to the participant then such deceit cannot be justified as being in the best interests of the participant. The Pearson Report recommended that those who volunteer to take part in medical research should receive compensation for any harm which occurs on a no-fault liability basis. However, this has not been implemented in law, though many researchers may well pay compensation on an ex-gratia basis.

Information given to those who donate eggs for IVF

It is a requirement that those who donate eggs or embryos to be used in *in vitro* fertilisation and other techniques should be given full information about the risks involved in what may be essentially a surgical procedure and requires drugs to induce super-ovulation. Since the donor obtains no personal benefit, she should therefore have a full understanding of all that is involved before giving consent, Schedule 3 of the Human Fertilisation and Embryology Act 1990 emphasises the importance of free and informed consent being given. The consent must be given in writing and cover the items specified in the schedule. Before the person gives consent she must

    a.   be given a suitable opportunity to receive proper counselling about the implications of taking the proposed steps; and

    b.   be provided with such relevant information as is proper.

Perhaps these provisions could be useful as an example of the principles to be followed in other information-giving situations.

Questions and Exercises

1. Distinguish in your practice the occasions on which you obtain written consent, consent by word of mouth and implied consent. Is there any consistency in the way in which consent is given?

2. Identify the occasions on which you have acted without the consent of the patient. What was the justification?

3. At present there is a gap in the law over the giving of consent on behalf of the mentally incompetent adult. How do you think this gap should be filled? Relatives? Professionals? Lawyers? Others? Give reasons for your answer.

4. The duty to inform the patient of risks is as much a part of the duty of care as that of treating the patient. Look at your practice of informing the patient and consider the extent to which it would comply with the law.

Chapter 5:
Access to Health Records

It comes as a surprise to many that until recently there was no legally recognised right for a patient to see his medical records. Even now there is no absolute right and access can be denied for several reasons.

Data Protection Act 1984

The first legal opportunity came about as a result of the Data Protection Act 1984. The Act was passed partly to prevent damage to our international trade which could have occurred if the United Kingdom were not to ratify the Council of Europe Convention for the Protection of Individuals with regard to Automatic Processing of Personal Data.

The Act only covered automatically processed information relating to individuals and at that time the vast proportion of medical reports were held in manual form and not computerised.

An individual is given the right at reasonable intervals and without undue delay or expense

1. to be informed by any Data User whether he holds personal data of which that individual is the subject, and

2. to access any such data held by a Data User, and

3. where appropriate to have such data corrected or erased.

Who owns the records?

Patients may consider that since their medical/health records are about them, then they are the first persons who would have right of access. However, this is not so. Historically there has been controversy over who owns the patient's medical records: doctors have claimed that since they write them, possibly with their own pens and ink, from confidences given by the patient, then they own them. This is not necessarily the situation, however. NHS records belong to the Secretary of State and the health authority members and the NHS Trusts acting in accordance with its delegated function have the right of ownership and therefore of disclosure, subject to law. Family Health Services Authorities can insist on GP records being returned to them when the patient dies or transfers to another GP and there is a contractual duty for the GP to keep appropriate records. Breach of this duty could make the GP liable to a hearing for breach of his terms and conditions of service, held by the Medical Services Committee of the FHSA.

Access to Medical Reports Act 1988

The next opportunity for a legal enforceable right of access came with the passing of the Access to Medical Reports Act 1988. This gave the right to an individual to have access to any medical report relating to him, which is to be or has been supplied by a medical practitioner for employment purposes or insurance purposes. It came into force on 1st January 1989.

Access to Health Records Act 1990

Finally, on November 1st 1991 Patients were given the right of access to their non-computerised health records. 'Health Records' is widely defined and consists of information relating to the physical or mental health of an individual who can be identified from that information and has been made by or on behalf of a health professional. Information which would be covered by the Data Protection Act is expressly excluded, so the two Acts—Access to Health Records Act 1990 and the Data Protection Act 1984—are complementary.

How is health professional defined?

Health professional is widely defined and includes most registered health professionals such as: doctors, dentists, opticians, pharmacists, nurses, midwives, health visitors, chiropodists, dietitians, occupational therapists, orthoptists, physiotherapists, clinical psychologists, psychotherapists or speech therapists and art or music therapists employed by a health service body. It does not however include social workers.

The Act gives a right of access to:

- the patient;
- a person authorised in writing to make an application on the patient's behalf;
- the person having parental responsibility for a child patient;
- someone appointed by the court to manage the affairs of an incompetent patient;
- or the personal representative of a patient where the patient has died;
- or any person having a claim arising out of the patient's death.

The rights of access include:

- being allowed to inspect the records;
- being given a copy of the record; and
- receiving an explanation of any terms which are unintelligible without an explanation,

The applicant can ask for records he believes to be inaccurate to be corrected. Inaccurate means 'incorrect, misleading or incomplete'.

The holder is not bound to comply with the request for correction if he believes the information is accurate, but in this case the holder must make a note on the relevant part of the records of the matters of which the applicant has complained.

Exclusion of right of Access:

These three enactments might seem to cover every aspect of the patient's right of access and give the patient a significant power. However, all three statutes have similar exclusion clauses which enable the patient to be denied this right.

A health professional (see previous page for the definition of this term) can exclude access where in the opinion of the holder access would disclose

i)   information likely to cause serious harm to the physical or mental health of the patient or of any other individual, or

ii) information relating to a third party who could be identified and has not given his consent to disclosure.

There is no statutory definition of 'serious harm to the physical or mental health' and until there are court cases where a refusal to permit access on these grounds is challenged by the patient, it is uncertain how these terms will be judicially interpreted.

Therapeutic privilege

The Act permits the existence of the 'therapeutic privilege' noted in the Sidaway dicta in the House of Lords for professionals to act paternalistically towards patients. There may of course be problems for patients in learning that they are terminally ill or suffering from a chronic condition, but one would hope that health professionals would work towards assisting patients to take this knowledge on board, rather than deny them the information. So it is a question of delaying the access to the information rather than preventing it entirely.

Some psychiatrists may consider that the therapeutic relationship which exists between the patient and the psychiatrist might be destroyed if the patient is permitted access. However, a request for access might indicate poor communication between professional and patient and feelings of mistrust from the latter. There may well be cases where patients have to be protected against information, and paternalism is therefore justifiable, especially in cases of psychiatric disorder and the debate illustrates the gap between those insisting on the patient's right to complete disclosure and those who defend the health professional's duty of care and duty to protect the patient, if necessary, from distressing information.

There are also powers of total exclusion of the right of access under the 1990 Act depending upon the kind of applicant.

For example, where the patient is a child there is no right of access to the child unless the holder of the records is satisfied that he/she is capable of understanding the nature of the application

Effect of right of access:

If patients make use of these statutory qualified rights of access, and it is likely that they will be encouraged to do so by patient representative organisations such as Action for Victims of Medical Accidents, Community Health Councils, Patients' Association, etc., then the existence of these rights might well have a significant effect on patient/professional relationships.

1. In the first place, professionals, especially doctors, will be deterred from writing defamatory or abusive opinions in the records, such as 'this neurotic mother', 'I hope I never see this patient again', 'this dollop', and these are examples taken from actual records. The advantage is that their negative opinions of such patients will not automatically be passed on to colleagues who subsequently care for the patient, who will examine the patient free from the prejudices of their colleagues.

2. Secondly, it is possible that knowing the patient could have access to his records might encourage some professionals to be more open and disclose information they might only, previously, have put in writing or told other professionals. Communication may improve. Professionals may increasingly respect the patient's autonomy and the patient's need to have full information about his condition including the fact that it was terminal or chronic.

   In some wards, for example, imaginative use (especially in the care of the mentally disordered) has been made of record keeping to involve the patient in commenting upon his care and making positive suggestions on his future care.

3. Thirdly, some doctors have expressed the view that they will be encouraged by the Act to develop a secondary system of records which are kept for their own benefit and are not available to the patient. However, the wide definition of health records would prevent this, since these supplementary, private records would also be subject to the access provisions. When this is realised, the standard of record keeping of all records may improve. It is not only medical records which are subject to the Act, but also nursing physiotherapy, dietetic, X-rays and any personal information relating to the physical or mental health which identifies that

individual. In other words, all health records made by or on behalf of a health professional are subject to the Act.

Nor can a professional hide behind jargon. S.3(3) of the Act states that 'where any information contained in a record or extract which is so allowed to be inspected, or a copy of which is so supplied, is expressed in terms which are not intelligible without explanation, an explanation of those terms shall be provided with the record or extract, or supplied with the copy'.

This sub-section could be interpreted as requiring an explanation if the terms are illegible and thus the professionals could not hide behind bad writing.

4.   The standard of record keeping should also improve because of the right of the patient to apply for the correction of the record if any information is inaccurate. An application for correction would initially be made to the holder of the records. However, if the holder fails to comply, an application can be made to the High Court or County Court for the holder to be ordered to comply.

Should there be restrictions on access?

There are grounds for believing that there is no justification for limiting the patient's right of access to his health records—either to protect third parties who have given information and do not want their involvement to be known by the patient—or even to protect the patient. However, not all professionals would support this. The exclusion does allow for individual needs and characteristics of the patient to be taken into account. In addition, the appeals mechanism ensures that there is a review of the withholding of records. Many practitioners are finding, even in the psychiatric field, that a more open policy on disclosure of information to the patient does have beneficial therapeutic effects. The nature of the disclosure and how it is handled becomes more important. There are ways of informing patients sensitively and sympathetically about bad news and it would be unfortunate if an absolute right of access were accompanied by callous cynical disclosure.

Disclosure of terminal illness—Japan

A Japanese high court ruled in November 1990 that doctors are NOT obliged to tell patients they are suffering from cancer. The family had alleged that had the patient and her family known she was suffering from cancer of the gall-bladder, and not gall-stones, then she would not have stopped visiting the hospital (since she believed she was not seriously ill and possibly would have been alive today). In Japan, surveys showed 8 out of 10 doctors in Japan lie to cancer patients. They give a diagnosis of a stomach ulcer, a vaginal cyst or gall-stones to avoid telling the truth.

However, on the other side of the coin, most Japanese patients, unaware that many cancers can be treated if caught early, prefer not to know. Cancer carries a great stigma in Japan, where it is the country's single biggest killer.

United Kingdom

In this country there is no settled policy that the patient should not be notified of a terminal illness. Often, in fact, nursing staff find that when they are caring for the elderly their relatives are unwilling for the patient to be notified of a terminal prognosis and prefer the professional staff to keep such information from the patient on the grounds that the patient would be incapable of coping with the information. Thus, the rule that the patient should be notified of confidential information and then gives consent to who else should be told is not followed (see Chapter 6). The exclusion of the right of access should be on stronger grounds than that the information would be upsetting. Serious harm should be shown.

The right of access to information and records is at the heart of the debate between paternalism and autonomy. At present, the law is a compromise: access is permitted, but can be refused if it is in the best interests of the patient himself or to protect a third person. It may be that improvements in communication and the emphasis on the patient's autonomy might eventually lead to an absolute right of access.

Questions and Exercises

1. Do you consider that the patient should have an absolute right of access to his health records?

2. How would you define serious harm for the purposes of the Access to Health Records Act?

3. Are there any conditions where you think the patient should always have access and never be denied it?

4. How has the Act affected your system of record keeping?

5. Can you identify ways in which the right of access could be of positive benefit both to the patient and to the staff?

6. What problems are caused administratively by this right of access? How could they be overcome?

Chapter 6:
The Right to Confidentiality

The duty to keep information confidential

When we turn to the right of the patient to insist that information concerning him/herself be kept confidential, there are very few cases where the patient has been successful in enforcing it—perhaps because once the sensitive information has been unlawfully passed on, there is little point in publicising it further by court action—or perhaps because patients are realistic in knowing there is extreme likelihood that the information will not be kept confidential.

Professional Codes of Conduct

The earliest medical codes recognised the doctor's duty to keep patient information confidential

> "Whatever I may see or hear in the course of treatment or even outside of the treatment in regard to the life of men, which on no account must spread abroad, I will keep to myself holding such things shameful to be spoken about."

and this is reiterated in the Code of Professional Conduct for nurses, midwives and health visitors produced by the United Kingdom Central Council of Nursing, Midwifery and Health Visiting. An advisory paper expands on the confidentiality issue further. This paper recommended the inclusion of a term requiring an employee to observe a patient's confidence to be included in the contract of employment and this is recommended by the Department of Health.

The duty to respect confidential information derives from several sources: it is part of the duty of care which arises at common law and follows from the professional/patient relationship; it arises from the contract of employment between employee and employer, and it may arise from statutory provision.

Exclusions to the duty:

However, the exclusions to the duty to maintain confidentiality are numerous, cause considerable confusion and are endangering the right of confidentiality itself.

Figure 10 shows the main exceptions to the duty of confidentiality.

Figure 10: Exceptions to the Duty of Confidentiality

1.	Consent of the patient.
2.	Interests of the patient.
3.	Court Order (a) Subpoena (b) Supreme Court Act 1981
4.	Statutory duty to disclose e.g. Road Traffic Act Prevention of Terrorism Acts Public Health Acts Misuse of Drugs Acts Police and Criminal Evidence Acts
5.	Public Interest

No right of privileged information recognised by the court.

The court does not recognise any privilege of a doctor or other health professional to refuse to provide information relating to the patient's personal records, and an order for production can be made before the issue of a writ in cases of personal injuries or death when the plaintiff or defendant is in possession of that information or after the case has commenced against a third party. During the hearing the judge has the right to subpoena witnesses who can be ordered to bring documents with them. Any rights of confidentiality are dependent upon the sensitivity of the judge or registrar in limiting both the information required to that which is relevant to an issue arising in the case and the disclosure of that information to the purposes required by the court.

Statutory duty to inform.

Some statutes require the passing on of otherwise confidential information—See Figure 10. The case of *Hunter v. Mann* is well known for a doctor's attempt to preserve patient confidentiality. The doctor failed to provide details of the patient who was injured in a road traffic accident as required under road traffic legislation and was fined £5.

Other legislation dealing with public health requires information relating to infectious diseases to be passed to the Community Medical Officer. AIDS and HIV-positive cases are covered by specific legislation.

The powers of the police and procedures to be followed to obtain personal health information or samples of body fluids are now the subject of statutory provision under the Police and Criminal Evidence Act 1984. A recent case emphasised that every factor required by the Act must exist before the disclosure of the records will be ordered. (*R. v. Central Criminal Court Ex parte Brown*, **Times**, 7 September 1992)

Disclosure with the consent of the patient

The patient himself can, of course, consent to the passing on of any confidential information and this consent would be a valid defence in an action for breach of confidentiality. Indeed, nurses report the difficulties of maintaining confidentiality when the patient declares his personal details, history, diagnosis and prognosis to the ward or even the world. This trend of public figures permitting the press to have the most intimate details of their health to be printed and announced may perhaps result from the pressure to maintain good public relations. The announcement of a member of the royal family entering hospital for a few days is usually followed by details as to the reason, plus a condition bulletin at frequent intervals given, hopefully, with the consent of the patient. The right to have the information kept confidential gives way to the pressure to tell all. At present there is no Privacy Act which makes the disclosure of private information an offence or actionable. Unless a duty to maintain confidentiality arises by contract of employment, common law duty of care or agreement between the parties, then the information can be disclosed to the world.

Release of information as a result of an implied consent by the patient took on an interesting twist in a recent Canadian case. The plaintiff was suing for alleged negligence and tried to prohibit the medical practitioner who was treating him from discussing his case with defence lawyers. The court held that he had impliedly consented to waive his right to confidentiality by bringing an action in which his medical condition is placed in issue. It is uncertain whether the same position would apply in this country and statutory provision exists to compel disclosure to parties within the case, but this does not cover discussions and consultations between the plaintiff's present medical practitioners and defence lawyers.

Disclosure in the public interest

The largest exception to the duty of confidentiality relates to the passing on of information in the interests of the patient or the public. The former would cover the necessary exchange of information between health professionals caring for the patient, or even to volunteers or other employees if they need to know that information to protect the health and safety of the patient. However, disclosure in the public interest has rarely been defined and is subject to great debate though it has been recognised by the courts and by the professions.

The public interest—a psychiatric case

In one case, (*W. v. Egdell*, 1989) a patient suffering from mental disorder obtained an independent medical opinion from a psychiatrist for the purpose of an application to a mental health review tribunal. This independent report advised against the discharge of the patient. The patient refused permission for the report to be sent to the hospital, but the doctor sent the report to the hospital and he recommended that it should be sent to the Home Secretary. The Home Secretary subsequently sent a copy of the report to the Tribunal. The patient then brought an action against the doctor, the hospital board, the Home Secretary, Secretary of State and the Tribunal to restrain them from using the document and alleging a breach of the duty of confidentiality. The court had to decide whether the disclosure was justified in the public interest and what was meant by that term. In the Court of Appeal it was said that:

> "A consultant psychiatrist who becomes aware, even in the course of a confidential relationship of information which leads him, in the exercise of what the court considers a sound professional judgement to fear that such decisions (relating to the discharge of patients) may be made on inadequate information and with a real risk of consequent danger to the public is entitled to take such steps as are reasonable in all the circumstances to communicate the grounds of his concern to the responsible authorities."

The difficulties with this decision on the nature of the public interest is that the patient had in the past killed 5 people and badly injured two others. It remains uncertain as to the extent that it can be applied to the non-psychiatric situation. Clearly a threat of serious harm would have to be established. In cases of extreme danger to the public it could be argued that there is even a duty on the professional to disclose information to the appropriate authorities.

AIDS and HIV

The issue is of disclosure in the public interest is seen starkly in relation to patients who are HIV-positive or suffer from AIDS. Should the public have the right to know of this condition—e.g. should parents of children at a school attended by an HIV or AIDS sufferer know of this condition? Should surgeons and other health professionals have the right to insist on the patient being tested before they undertake their care?

There has been a recent case on the issue (*X v. Y and others*, 1988). Two general practitioners were diagnosed as suffering from AIDS and were receiving treatment but they continued in their general practice work. Information was given to a journalist by a health service employee about their condition as well as the medical records. The health authority applied for an injunction to prevent the disclosure of any further information in the press and disclosure of the name of the employee. The court held that the public interest in preserving confidentiality of hospital records identifying actual or potential AIDS sufferers outweighed the public interest in the freedom of the press to publish such information, because the victims of the disease ought not to be deterred by fear of discovery from going to hospital for treatment, and free and informed public debate about AIDS could take place without publication of the confidential information acquired by the defendants. The health authority was therefore able to obtain an injunction. However, the court did not agree to an order to disclose the name of the employee because it had not been established that disclosure was necessary to prevent a crime as required by the Contempt of Court Act 1981.

There has recently been considerable public debate over whether there should be a right to insist upon an individual undergoing an HIV/AIDS test—not so much an issue over consent to treatment since at present there is no known successful treatment, but an issue over whether a person can keep his health status unknown even to himself.

Declarations

The declaration of the rights of people with HIV and AIDS states

> "People with HIV and AIDS have the right to privacy and in respect of this right, we believe that:
> information about the HIV status of any person should be kept confidential to that person and their appointed health and social carers (except where anonymous information is given to a public body for the purpose of studying the epidemiology of HIV);
> information should not be disclosed to a third party about a person's HIV status without that person's consent."

Uncertainty of the legal position

At present the absence of statutory rights and the lack of clarity on the common law do not give these provisions legal standing.

In spite of attempts by professional organisations and registration bodies to define what is meant by release of confidential information in the public interest, this is not the law. There is no statutory definition and the few cases which exist are so specific to particular circumstances that it is both difficult and dangerous to define with clarity when confidential information can justifiably be disclosed in the public interest.

Situations such as telling the Vehicle Licensing Authority about someone known to be an uncontrolled epileptic, notifying the patient's spouse that the patient has a venereal disease, are often fascinating for the philosopher and student of ethics but frustrating for those requiring to know the legal situation.

Occupational Health Departments:

The problems are seen particularly in the field of the occupational health professional. One of the principles of their profession is the maintenance of confidentiality between employee and the occupational health department and there are suggested codes to protect this principle. However, these codes are not the law of the land and there is no certainty as to what information respecting the employee's health is protected from disclosure. Similar problems beset the occupational health service in Higher Education and probably in other spheres of work, education and leisure activity. The Department of Health/Welsh Office is currently preparing a Code of Confidentiality. The delay in its production indicates the difficulties in obtaining a consensus view over what are the justifiable exceptions to the duty to maintain confidentiality.

Conclusions

As long as these uncertainties exist, the right of the patient to prevent unauthorised disclosure is severely limited and the protection of the patient's interests and privacy rests upon the attitudes of health professionals, employers, the media and ultimately the general public. The emphasis they place upon the protection of confidential information as opposed to the protection of the public interest will determine the nature of the legislation which will eventually be enacted.

Questions and exercises

1. Consider the extent to which the duty of confidentiality is broken in hospitals. How do you think that the duty could be enforced?

2. Have you ever encountered a conflict between the duty to the patient and the public interest? How was it resolved?

3. Which other health professionals do you think would be justified in having access to the records of the patient in your particular specialty?

4. Identify those occasions on which you consider the public interest will always take preference over the interests of the patient.

Chapter 6:
Other Rights

There are other rights which should be considered. These are shown in figure 11.

Figure 11: Other rights which shall be considered.

1.	To obtain a second opinion.
2.	To have privacy.
3.	To be treated with courteousness.
4.	To have one's complaints investigated.

1. To have a second medical opinion

Whilst this right is included in the patient's charter it is one which is difficult to enforce unless it can be proved that the doctor (usually general practitioner) was not following the approved standard of care (i.e. The Bolam Test) in failing to refer the patient to a second-opinion doctor. Similarly, although a patient could request that the consultant he is seeing in secondary care should refer him to a similar or different specialist, he has no right in law to insist upon such a referral. Normally, of course, the doctor would be happy to make the referral if he was concerned that the patient was not happy with the advice or diagnosis, and treatment that he had been given. However, it is in those difficult areas where there is a refusal to refer that enforcement is unclear. If any reasonable doctor would in that situation have recommended that a second opinion should be sought then there would be evidence of negligence. In other cases where negligence cannot be shown enforcing this right other than through the complaints machinery is not possible.

Internal Market:

The situation may become more complex with the establishment of the internal market. In effect, the second opinion means two lots of purchases for fund-holding general practitioners and there may well be a reluctance on the part of GPs. who have the budget to purchase secondary services to buy another consultation for their patients, if they themselves are happy with the initial opinion.

Second opinion for mentally detained patients:

The Mental Health Act 1983 requires a second-opinion doctor to be appointed in those situations when a detained patient is incapable of giving consent or refuses to give consent to electro-convulsive therapy, or where the detained patient has been receiving medication for three months and either refuses to give consent to medication or is incapable of giving consent.

Outside the NHS

The above discussion obviously refers to referrals within the NHS. There is no reason why there cannot be referrals outside the NHS, i.e. to doctors in private practice, provided the patient is prepared to pay for the consultation. It is, of course, customary to obtain the approval of the doctor currently advising the patient. The advantage of this prior approval is that he can make available his records to the new doctor and any diagnostic test that he has arranged need not necessarily be repeated, since the results can also be made available.

2. To have privacy

Anyone who has worked or been a patient on a Florence Nightingale Ward with beds either side of a long, narrow room will know how impossible it would be to give patients privacy. Patients do have a right to confidentiality (see Chapter 6) and so they could insist that they are not interviewed in a public place where they could be overheard. However, the curtains around the bed provide little noise proofing and staff, particularly doctors on ward rounds, are not always sensitive to the patient's need for privacy. NHS patients have no right to single-room accommodation. Rules of public decency would normally be respected, including providing separate toilet facilities for men and women, but there is no right for a patient to insist on being cared for in single-sex accommodation. Increasingly, the need for maximum occupancy of beds and flexibility of use may mean that men and women are cared for in the same rooms.

There is at present no Right to Privacy Act so unless patients can show a breach of confidentiality they have no redress for what they regard as an invasion of their privacy.

3. To be treated with courtesy

Discourtesy which amounts to a breach of the peace or an assault, where a trespass to the person is feared, is actionable in a court of law—either criminal or civil depending on the circumstances.

Conduct less extreme than this may well be the subject of a complaint and if substantiated could lead to disciplinary action by the employer against the member of staff concerned. Professional conduct proceedings could also take place against the practitioner if the conduct amounts to the type of misconduct with which they have jurisdiction to deal. Certainly the Professional Conduct Committee of the UKCC would be concerned to investigate any such allegations against a registered nurse, midwife or health visitor.

4. To have one's complaints investigated

The Hospital Complaints Procedure Act 1985 places a statutory duty upon the Secretary of State to ensure that a complaints procedure was set up in each hospital.

The Secretary of State has asked for this procedure also to be available in the community.

There is a formal and informal procedure for complaints about the services supplied by the Family Health Service Authorities (FHSA), i.e. general practitioners, dentists, and pharmacists.

In the event of the complaint not being appropriately investigated there are appeal mechanisms. The Health Service Commissioner (The Ombudsman) has the power to investigate any complaints (excluding clinical matters, staff complaints and FHSA complaints) if the complainant remains dissatisfied after the health authority has considered the complaint.

Patients who are detained under the provisions of the Mental Health Act also have the right to complain to the Mental Health Act Commission which can consider all complaints and is not confined to non-clinical matters.

The Health Service Commissioner also has the power to hear complaints about the functioning of the Mental Health Act Commission.

Basic rights of the citizen:

In addition, for those patients who are detained under the provisions of the Mental Health Act and who are kept in special hospitals, or regional secure units or other accommodation for the mentally disordered, other possible rights should be considered. These are shown in figure 12 (overleaf).

Most people would agree that patients who have lost their freedom because of a mental disorder should not be punished for this. Even if the safety of the public or of the patient him/herself requires the patient to be detained, it does not follow that he/she should therefore lose all the other rights that a citizen enjoys and which are listed in figure 12. Many more could be added.

Sexual Relations

For the most part the list is not controversial. However, when we move into the area of sexual relationships, there would be no consensus that detained patients are entitled to have sex. Difficulties arise in deciding if this right exists in relation to fellow patients. It is an issue which causes concern in

Figure 12:   Basic Rights of Citizens

1.   The right to use a telephone.

2.   The right to have access to a telephone.

3.   The right to receive visitors.

4.   The right to receive mail.

5.   The right to have clothing.

6.   The right to have food.

7.   The right to sleep.

8.   The right to have pain killers and treatment.

9.   The right to have company and not be secluded.

10. The right to smoke.

11. The right to have access to books, paper, writing materials and newspapers.

12. The right to post letters.

13. The right to see T. V.

14. The right to smoke.

15. The right to have exercise.

16. The right to be treated with dignity and respect.

community homes for the non-detained mentally handicapped, especially where there might be a possibility that a female patient/resident is not capable of giving a valid consent and is therefore being exploited. It can cause even more difficulty where patients are detained. Should staff enable detained patients to have sexual relationships on mixed wards? What of homosexual relationships? Would a ward be described as a public place so that any such activity would be regarded as criminal under our existing laws? Or are the bedrooms and bathrooms to be regarded as non-public places, so that if the acts take place there by consenting adults then they are not illegal? Yet what is meant by consent in the context of a locked ward where power and pressure groups between patients are common? These are very real problems on which the staff need to have guidance and policies.

Sexual Relationships with non-patients

A further problem exists in relationship to sexual relations with non-patients. If a detained patient is married, what rights has the spouse to ask to come and stay the night to continue the marital relationship? The question has been considered for those in prison but has not been explored for those who are detained under Mental Health Laws. At present, many managers of secure accommodation would conclude that to provide such facilities would create an impossible security risk and therefore would not be permitted. Such a blanket policy might not however always be based on the truth.

Rights of the detained patient

Of the rights of the citizen which are set out in figure 12, most would be provided as part of the duty of care. Certainly, the right to painkillers and treatment would be covered by the right to a reasonable standard of care discussed in Chapter 3. It could also be assumed that the standard of care as judged by the Bolam Test would include a reasonable standard of living: food, clothing, society, recreation, exercise and communications with the outside world would all be included in that.

The difficulty is that they are only enforceable, as was seen in Chapter 3, through civil court action where harm can be proved. As was pointed out in the introductory chapter, there is in this country no Bill of Rights to which a detained person can refer. The European Convention on Human Rights is not directly enforceable through our courts; litigants would still have to go to Strasbourg and this can be a slow and costly battle.

For detained patients there are no minimum standards of care laid down in the legislation. It is forbidden for postal packets to be withheld from them unless the patient is in a special hospital and it is necessary to do so in the interests of the safety of the patient or for the protection of other persons. The provisions covering treatment for mental disorder are comprehensive. However, provisions relating to the other aspects of care

are described in the Code of Practice and this does not have statutory force. Commissioners in their visits can comment adversely when the conditions in which the patient is detained fall below those recommended in the Code. However, they do not have any powers of enforcement. Patients are still found deprived of their pyjamas during the day, patients are still secluded unnecessarily, and very few have an automatic right of access to a telephone.

Questions and Exercises.

1. Are there any other rights which you would regard as essential for the patient's well-being?

2. Do you think that a distinction between the rights of the detained patient and the rights of the non-detained patient is meaningful?

3. Do you think that the law should recognise a right to privacy?

4. Do you think that patients should have the right to be involved in ward management decisions through patients' forums?

Chapter 7:
Patients' Rights and the Patient's Charter

Citizen's and Patient's Charters

In July 1992 the Citizen's Charter was published and the basic provisions can be seen in figure 13.

Figure 13a: Citizen's Charter

Every Citizen is entitled to expect:

        Standards

        Openness

        Information

        Choice

        Non-Discrimination

        Accessibility

        A Complaints Procedure/Redress

Figure 13b: Aims of the Citizen's Charter (July 1991)

1. Better quality in every public service.

2. Give people more choice.

3. Ensure that people are notified of the kind of service they can expect to receive.

4. Ensure that people know what to do if things go wrong.

This was followed by the Patient's Charter with different editions being published by the different parts of the United Kingdom. Common to them all are the sections shown in figure 14.

Figure 14: Patient's Charter

Patients can expect:

a.   to be treated with care, consideration, and respect.

b.   to receive the right kind of service at the right place.

c.   to be given the opportunity to talk about and to help choose care and treatment.

d.   to have information in English, Welsh and other languages.

e.   that relatives and friends will be informed about progress of treatment subject to the patient's wishes.

Rights in relation to   •   Doctors
                             •   Dentists
              and   •   the Hospital Service.

Since then, local health authorities have been asked to prepare their own charters for their patients and an example of one is shown in figure 15 (overleaf).

Enforceability

How do these provisions affect the law? Are they legally enforceable? At present it appears that the Charters do not give any legally enforceable rights in health care though there is provision in some of the other service industries such as British Rail for financial compensation to be made available for failures in provision.

Minimum waiting times

For example, the patient's charter sets a minimum time within which a patient should receive surgery. If the patient has waited longer than that, what remedies does he have? From the cases discussed in Chapter 2, it is unlikely that he would have an enforceable action in the courts unless he can show great unreasonableness by the authorities in the allocation of

Figure 15:   Example of Local Patient's Charter

You have the right to expect prompt, courteous and considerate service

- to be addressed as you wish.

- to receive adequate notice of your appointment in hospital.

- to know the names of those involved in caring for you.

- to be advised of any delays/waiting times.

- to be advised about any proposed treatment; to be aware of any risks involved or alternative treatment available, before you decide whether you will agree to any treatment.

- to be asked whether or not you wish to take part in any medical research or student training, and to know that your decision will not affect the care you receive.

- to receive timely advice of discharge or transfer to enable transport, domestic or continuing care arrangements to be made.

- to be treated in clean and comfortable surroundings

- to make your opinions known about the care you have received.

- to receive respectful and prompt attention to any complaint you should have occasion to make.

- to receive information in English, Welsh or another language.

- to have access to your health records under certain circumstances.

resources and the determination of priorities. Unless he can establish medical negligence, he cannot sue successfully for compensation in the civil courts. He does not personally have the right to seek treatment in the private sector and invoice the health authority for that care. He might be referred to another hospital outside the catchment area, but only if he has the consent of his local purchasing authority who would have to pay the costs. If he belongs to a GP fund-holding practice, his GP might arrange for him to be cared for outside the catchment area by another provider. These are not however legally enforceable rights which belong to the patient.

Value of the Charters

Is the patient's charter then all hype?

In one sense the answer could probably be yes. The patient's charter can be seen in the context of the consumerist movement which began with the Griffith's report in to the management of the NHS. Griffiths was the managing director of Sainsbury and his recommendations on the general management within the NHS were accompanied by the view that saw patients as customers or consumers. There is however a huge difference. The NHS patient has no contractual relationship with the supplier of services, unlike his counterpart in retail (and as we shall see in Chapter 8 unlike his counterpart in the private health-care sector). The protection given in the Sale of Goods and Services legislation is not available to the NHS customer. There is no equivalent of 'not of the essence', 'not fit for its purpose', 'making time of the essence', which are well established in consumer law. Instead, the NHS patient has to rely upon the Bolam Test and the laws of negligence and can only sue when harm has occurred. The charter does not give any additional legal rights.

Lost opportunity

A golden opportunity was lost in the National Health Service and Community Care Act 1990. This Act saw the implementation of the 'internal market concept' through the establishment of NHS Trusts who as providers of services could establish NHS agreements with health service bodies who acted as purchasers. Similar agreements have been set up between directly managed units (DMUs) and the purchasers. In the field of general practice, the fund-holding group practices take over the role of purchasing secondary services from providers on behalf of their patients, as well as being providers to them. These NHS agreements between purchaser and provider do not give rise to contractual liabilities or rights. (S.4). There is therefore no way in which these agreements can be enforced. In the event of a dispute, the Secretary of State can intervene himself or appoint an adjudicator.

No enforceable rights

The patient has no enforceable rights under these NHS agreements. The golden opportunity which was lost in the National Health Service and Community Care Act 1990 is the failure to include the patient in this internal market. Health Service bodies purchase services on behalf of the patient. The patient has no personal say in this agreement. Until a formula is drafted which includes the patient in the internal market, consumerism and patients' rights are likely to continue to be unevenly recognised across the country. Give the patient contractual rights, give the patient purchasing power, or give the patients power to enforce both statutory duties and the NHS agreements and the situation would be revolutionised.

Standard setting and patient rights

There is however another way of looking at the question. It is possible to see the standard setting initiative of the patient's charter as being at the heart of the internal market. If purchasers insist that providers negotiate agreements which ensure that the terms of the patient's charter are included and if purchasers monitor the performance of the providers and look at the extent to which the provisions of the charter have been implemented, then the charter may become effective in influencing the standards of health care which exist. The patient would benefit if the standards are met but if this does not happen the patient can only complain.

For example, there is a statutory requirement that after a mentally disordered person has been arrested by a policeman in a public place under S. 136 of the Mental Health Act, the patient must be seen by a registered medical officer and a social worker. Some purchasing health authorities have set down target times by which the visit by the responsible medical officer to the place of safety must be made and expect the provider of the service to monitor this provision. This kind of term within the service agreement enables targets to be set and monitored to ensure appropriate standards of care are provided. Similarly the NHS agreements can include reference to the Professional Codes of Conduct and the Code of Practice issued by the Department of Health in relation to the Mental Health Act provisions. It will then become a term of the NHS agreement that the provider and its staff will be expected to comply with these codes and standards.

Standard setting in relation to all aspects of health care with clearly definable targets has developed within the context of quality assurance and it thus becomes easier to ascertain the extent to which patients' rights are being met. Enforcement will however rest with individual purchasers and not with individual patients whose only recourse at present is the law of negligence.

Other Charters and Declarations of Rights

The citizen's charter and the patient's charter are not the only charters which have been published over recent years. There have been a spate of documents produced by specialist groups and some are shown in figure 16.

Figure 16: Examples of Organisations which have produced charters or declarations of customer's rights

- Code of Banking Practice – Lloyds Bank

- Business Banking Charter – Midlands Bank

- Kwik Fit Code of Practice

- Water Boards

- British Telecom

- Electricity Boards

- Passenger Charter – British Rail

- Commitment to Customers – British Gas

- Victims' Charter

- Education – A Charter for Parents

For the most part, however, these constitute statements as to how these pressure groups would like the law to be changed. They do not necessarily recite the actual law. In the light of earlier sections, it should be possible for you to decide which statements actually cover rights which are in existence now and which statements refer to so-called rights which have no legal force.

Questions and exercises

1. Draw up a charter for the patients in the specialty in which you work. How many of the clauses which you have written cover rights which are already legally enforceable?

2. Do you think there would be any benefit if this country had a Bill of Rights for all patients which had statutory force? If so what are the essential clauses which you would wish to see included?

3. Obtain a copy of the patient's charter. How many of the clauses are already implemented in relation to the patients for whom you care? What needs to be done to implement the others? How does the charter provided by your local health authority compare with the national charter?

4. Professional responsibility and accountability probably are of greater significance in the protection of the rights of the patient than any other provision. Do you agree and if so what support do professionals require to fulfil their responsibilities?

Chapter 8:
Patients' Responsibilities

Whilst the emphasis is on the rights of the patient it is important for the nurse to be aware of the responsibilities of the patient. These are set out in figure 17a. Figure 17b sets out the sanctions which are available.

Figure 17a: Patients' Responsibilities

1.	To inform staff of medical history, known contra-indications and relevant family information.
2.	To carry out instructions on treatment and care responsibly and carefully, or inform staff if this has not been done.
3.	To keep appointments or give advance notice of inability to attend.
4.	To obey hospital/clinic rules.
5.	To be considerate towards other patients and staff.
6.	To report complaints.

Figure 17b: Staff sanctions in the event of the responsibilities not being observed

1.	Only through the concept of contributory negligence if harm arises.
2.	As above.
3.	As above
4.	Through law relating to trespassers and power to evict.
5.	Probably not enforceable unless conduct amounts to a breach of the peace or a public-order offence.
6.	No remedial action or investigation is likely to be taken

What is their basis in law?

The contractual position.

The NHS patient—No contract. There is no contract between the patient and the health professional in the NHS or between the patient and the health authority whether purchaser or provider. This is because there is no consideration which passes between patient and provider. Even when charges are levied for services, these do not form the basis of a contract. Prescription charges, for example, often bear little relationship to the cost of the drugs being prescribed. The drugs are sometimes very much cheaper than the payment being made by the patient and at other times very much more expensive. The patient cannot claim that he has contractual entitlements to NHS care. Nor, however, can the professionals or health authorities claim that the patient has contractual duties towards them. It is not possible therefore to argue that the responsibilities of the patient derive from the law of contract.

Contributory Negligence

Responsibilities derive from the civil law and the concept of contributory negligence. If the patient were to bring a claim for compensation and if it were to be established that the patient had failed to notify the staff of important information, or the patient had failed to follow the instructions, then it might be held that his claim should be reduced by the extent to which he has added to the harm that he has suffered.

An example

For example, a patient might leave the accident and emergency department with his arm in plaster and be given a leaflet instructing him to return to hospital if there is unusual swelling or pain in the arm or if he has difficulties moving his fingers. These symptoms might occur but be ignored by the patient. If, subsequently, the patient has to have his arm amputated and sues for compensation then it could be argued that he must share some, if not all, of the responsibility for what has occurred. Obviously liability will depend on the exact circumstances. Did the staff make it clear to the patient how important those instructions were? Would the amputation have occurred anyway as a result of other causes?

The law of contributory negligence

The concept of contributory negligence derives from the law that a person who is bringing an action for compensation must bear some responsibility for the harm which has occurred if he has failed to take reasonable care of himself and is therefore partly to blame. If this failure can be proved then the amount of compensation can be reduced to reflect the extent of the plaintiff's (the person bringing the action) blame. Sometimes, there could be almost 100% responsibility and therefore the plaintiff would receive no compensation. On other occasions, the blame attributable to the plaintiff would be regarded as so insignificant that it can be disregarded completely. In car accidents, for example, where the innocent person has not been wearing a seat belt and this failure has resulted in his suffering greater injuries than would otherwise have been the case, the compensation payable to him for his injuries might be reduced by between 15 to 25%.

It follows therefore that the patient has a responsibility to take reasonable care of himself. Staff should be able to rely upon that. Obviously, the law takes into account the age and maturity of the patient and any physical or mental disabilities which impede him. Children can not be expected to be as careful of themselves as an adult. Where staff know the patient to be unable to understand instructions, then further precautions must be taken to ensure that the patient is appropriately cared for.

Expectations of the patient

What can be reasonably expected from the patient?

The following actions could probably be expected and failure by the patient to take them if they cause additional harm to the patient could be regarded as contributory negligence:

1. Following the instructions of the professional staff in relation to any treatment recommended.

2. Informing the staff of any contra-indications known to the patient before treatment is recommended. In addition, any information relating to the patient's own history or family medical history could be of assistance in deciding on diagnosis or treatment. Being prepared to answer questions and provide information which is relevant to the care and treatment.

3. Notifying the staff of any adverse effects of the treatment.

4. Carrying out any other instructions in relation to diet, exercise, smoking and life styles.

5. Keeping appointments and notifying staff if these cannot be kept.

What if the patient fails to obey these instructions?

Failure by the patient to follow the instructions does not mean that the staff can consider their duty to the patient as at an end. For example, if a patient makes it clear that he/she does not on religious grounds wish to have a blood transfusion, this would not justify any act of negligence by the staff. They would still have a legal duty to take all reasonable care of the patients subject to that restriction on their activities. If a patient with a severe cardiac condition still insists on smoking, this does not mean that the staff can discontinue caring for him, even though they might find the patient's attitude and actions repugnant.

Are there any other responsibilities of the patient?

The above responsibilities of the patient relate to those actions which would affect the patient obtaining full compensation were he to bring an action for negligence. However, if there is no action for negligence then there is no way in which the law takes account of the patient's conduct and since staff cannot refuse to treat patients who ignore instructions there is no way of insisting that the patients act responsibly.

There are other actions which morally would be considered to be part of the patient's conduct but failure to follow these are unlikely to affect any compensation awarded should negligence occur. These include the expectation that patients will be respectful of staff, polite, non-abusive, understanding of difficulties and therefore prepared to wait if other, more seriously ill patients need to take priority. In extreme situations, some of these could be enforced through our laws relating to breach of the peace and public order and police are sometimes called into an accident and emergency department to deal with abusive patients and relatives. In less extreme cases, staff have an expectation that patients will act courteously and politely, but this is not enforceable.

Trespassing

In the hospital context, difficult patients could be asked to leave the premises and if they refuse to leave, they become trespassers. The occupier is entitled to use all reasonable means to evict a trespasser. Again, this action would only be taken in very extreme circumstances. In the community, the reverse is the case and the patient or occupier could ask a community health worker to leave and the health worker would have to go.

Visiting rules

In the hospital context, it would be possible to enforce rules relating to which foods and drinks could be brought into hospital through the occupier's right to set down the terms on which any one is allowed on to the premises. For example, if the bringing into hospital of alcoholic beverages is forbidden, and this rule is ignored by relatives, then they could be asked to leave taking their drink with them. If the patient also refuses to obey similar rules or rules relating to smoking, it could be made clear that he can only continue to remain in hospital if he obeys the rules laid down by the occupier. This is because in law the patient and the relatives would be classified as visitors, and it is open to the occupier to lay down the terms on which the visitor is entitled to come onto the premises.

Dealing with rudeness and discourtesy

Is there then no limit to the rudeness and the discourtesy which a health worker would have to accept and continue to care for the patient? The court had to consider this question in a case where the patient was suffering from a chronic condition and was being cared for by the husband. He was so abusive to the staff who attended to her that in the end they withdrew their services from the patient. The husband then brought an action to enforce specific performance of the statutory duties. He failed in his action. The court held that staff could not be expected to continue to care for the patient in such circumstances. This is of course an extreme situation and services would not be withdrawn from a patient without considerable debate and warning. (*R. v. Hillingdon HA* ex parte *Wyatt*, 1977)

Reporting complaints

Another responsibility of the patient could be said to be the duty that once a matter for concern or complaint has arisen, to report it to the appropriate person to ensure that it can be properly investigated. Many patients might prefer to do nothing rather than cause an upset and perhaps cause distress to those staff to whom they are extremely grateful. However it could be said that there is a duty on the patient to report concerns to management so that it has the opportunity of improving the situation. The duty is not legally enforceable in law, except that the Health Service Commissioner will not investigate a complaint unless it has already been reported to the management who have had an opportunity to investigate it. Only if the patient continues to be dissatisfied can the Health Service Commissioner then investigate it.

Agreements within a behavioural modification programme and the NHS patient

Even though the NHS patient does not have a contractual relationship with the health service body providing care, agreements are sometimes drawn up which purport to bind the patient. These are often in the context of the treatment for mental illness or in the care of those with a learning disability. They are also used in the treatment of those with addictions. A typical agreement is shown in figure 18 (see Page 74).

What is the legal significance of these agreements? Are they binding upon the patient?

Requirements for a binding contract

For an agreement to be recognised by the courts as having contractual validity and therefore for the terms to be enforceable against both parties the following requirements are essential:

1. There should be a complete agreement by parties having the competence (i.e. mental capacity) to make such an agreement.

2. There should be consideration passing from the one party in return for the fulfilment of the promise of performance by the other party.

3. There must be an intention to create legal relationships as a consequence of the agreement.

Can these three elements be said to exist in the context of an agreement in the care and treatment of illness or disability?

a. The agreement.

In these circumstances, the agreement is usually clear and comprehensive. An offer to take part in a therapy programme is made to the patient/client and accepted by him/her. The mental capacity of the patient to make such an agreement is not always verified and if a patient who is suffers from intermittent mental disorder makes an agreement whilst mentally capable to do so, is the agreement binding upon him when he becomes mentally disordered? This point will be discussed below. The capacity of some of those suffering from a mental handicap may not be sufficient for them to bind themselves in this way. On the other hand there may be some patients who do have the capacity and are able to enter into such an agreement. In the fields of alcohol and drug addiction, clear terms may be set down as to the conditions on which patients can be taken onto a particular programme.

b. Consideration

The requirement for consideration means that something must be given in exchange for the performance of the promise. It need not necessarily be money. It could be the performance of a task. A promise to pay another person a sum of money is not binding unless the recipient does something for the performance of the promise. That is why such gifts have to be made by deed which can then be enforced. What does the patient do in exchange for being taken onto the programme? Certainly within the NHS context no money changes hands. Could it be said that the mere fact that the patient undergoes some of the tasks set in the behaviour programme constitutes consideration? Possibly but as soon as the patient changes his mind and withdraws from the programme nothing can then be binding upon him. In drug/alcohol modification programmes, a patient who fails to follow the rules about abstaining from drugs or alcohol could be taken off the programme and would have no right to insist on being reinstated. In this sense, the agreement is effective. If the only reason he is in hospital is his presence on the programme, then he could justifiably be discharged and if there were no other condition requiring treatment he could be ordered to leave the premises.

It should be made clear, however, that consideration can not consist of doing something that one is already obliged to perform. Patients suffering from learning disabilities who are included in a behavioural modification programme could not be deprived of food or clothing or sleep or other necessities of life since the health service body providing their care would be regarded as having a duty to give those to the patient anyway. The rewards should relate to things over and above those facilities and amenities which should already be provided.

c. Intention to create legal relations.

Even if there is a clear agreement between the parties and there is something which could be legally regarded as consideration, the agreement would still not be recognised by the courts as one which would be binding upon the parties unless there was an intention to create a legal relationship.

In commercial contracts, the presumption is that there is such an intention, but the parties can specifically deny that fact. In domestic matters, the presumption is that there is no such intention but the parties could incorporate such an intention in the agreement. For example, an agreement to pay children pocket money in exchange for their making the beds would not regarded as having any intention of creating legal relationships and would not be regarded by the courts as enforceable.

It is likely that the agreements drawn up by patients and staff would be regarded by the courts as comparable to domestic agreements and therefore would not be enforced by them. What if such a term were to be included? The courts would then look very closely at the other requirements to be satisfied that the parties did have the necessary capacity and that there is consideration.

Agreements overriding patients' consent

What is the significance in law of those agreements which have been drawn up by doctors whereby the patient agrees to undergo treatment at a time when they are mentally well and in this document they sign that they give consent to treatment being given when they are mentally disordered and at the time of administration are refusing to take it. They also agree in this document to give a certain period of notice—perhaps 48 hours before cancelling the agreement. If in reliance of the patient's signature to such a document, treatment is given forcibly against the patient's wishes, would the document protect the professional staff against an action for trespass to the person? An example is given in figure 18 (overleaf).

Such a question does not seem to have come before the courts. The Power of Attorney Act whereby a person appointed an agent to act in relation to his affairs stated that the agency ended if the appointer became mentally disordered. Since this is often the very time that an agent is required the Enduring Powers of Attorney Act was passed which enabled

**Figure 18: An attempt at limiting the patient's free subsequent
refusal to have treatment**

I, ... being mentally competent know that there are
occasions when I become mentally disordered and at such times I
refuse treatment which is in my best interests. I therefore request
my responsible medical officer Dr . . . ., to ignore my refusal
to take recommended treatment when I am mentally disordered
and continue to administer such treatment against my will. I
hereby agree to give at least 48 hours notice of my intentions to
terminate this consent.

the agency to continue and not end if mental disorder occurred. However,
very strict procedures have to be followed for an enduring power to be
created. It is not thought that this act could apply to treatment and health
care and therefore a binding consent to treatment could not be covered by
these statutory provisions.

Even in the absence of statutory provision, could the contract be seen
as valid at common law?

The answer in relation to patients detained under the provisions of the
Mental Health Act 1983 is probably 'NO'. Such a contract would drive a
horse and cart through the detailed provisions for protecting patients
against compulsory treatment when they either refuse consent or are
incapable of consenting. Second-opinion doctors must examine the patient
and agree with the proposed treatment. Requirements in relation to the
documentation which must be kept are stringent and must be monitored.

It is doubtful if such a contract would be seen as binding upon the
informal patient. Detention provides considerable statutory protection for
those compelled to have treatment and the informal patient would not have
this protection. However, the point has still to be tested in court. In the
meantime professionals would be wise not to rely on such documents.

Failure to keep appointments without prior notification

As pressures for improved efficiency increase, the failure of the patient to
attend an out-patient clinic without prior notification of that possibility can
cause a waste of staff time and therefore an inefficient use of resources. As
fees have been levied for health services, e.g. dentists, some practitioners
have charged patients for their failure to attend. Where fees are not
payable, this sanction is not, of course, available but there are suggestions
that some sanctions should be available if it is thought that patients misuse
the services in some way.

In the private sector, of course, fees for failure to attend are well
established and might be payable even when the client has given advanced
notice.

See figure 19 for action which staff can take to encourage patients to be more responsible and figure 20 for the limits of their action.

Figure 19: Action staff can take to obtain greater responsibility from patients

1.	Leaflets/written instructions/written advice against premature discharge.
2.	Warnings about contributory negligence.
3.	Rules relating to visiting and in-patient stay in patient/ relative information handbooks.

Figure 20: Action staff cannot take to impose responsibility upon patients

1.	Staff cannot withdraw care.
2.	Staff cannot impose fines.
3.	Staff cannot lower standards of care to which the patient is entitled.

The private fee-paying patient

All that has been said above applies to the private patient who is receiving care outside the NHS. However, in addition there is a contractual relationship between the private patient and those providing services. Sometimes the patient may be paying personally, more often the fees are paid through insurance cover and the insurance company may or may not manage the premises on which the care is given. This contractual relationship is missing in the relationship between the NHS patient and the health service body providing treatment and care.

There would be in this relationship between private patient and the provider of care those three elements discussed above which are essential for an agreement to be valid in law.

The contract permits the inclusion of terms which cover not only the responsibilities to the patient but also any responsibilities owed by the patient. The contract could therefore cover all the responsibilities of the patient in relation to the disclosure of relevant information, and in following instructions and also the conduct which would be expected of a patient. Such contractual terms would be binding on the patient. If, however, the patient were to be injured or suffer as a result of an act of negligence, the liability of the staff would not be excluded as a result of the patient's failures because of the effect of the Unfair Contract Terms Act. The failures would however be taken into account in assessing any contributory negligence as discussed above.

Questions and exercises

1. At present there is a distinction between the legal position of the NHS patient and the private patient. Can you think of any ways in which the NHS patient can be given as much protection as the private patient? Are there any advantages (apart from financial) which the NHS patient has compared to the private patient?

2. How can the nurse make it clear that the patient has responsibilities as well as the nurse for his health and well-being?

3. In extreme situations the patient could be asked to leave the ward. Identify from your own experience the events which could rise to such a request being made. What procedures and guidelines do you think should be set down to ensure that the patients' rights are protected?

4. The list of responsibilities identified here does not necessarily cover every possibility. Are there any others which you consider important?

Chapter 9:
Conclusion

Perhaps, however, the emphasis of this book is wrong. Perhaps patients' rights and the law are wrongly juxtaposed. After all, what can the law do—it can only provide a remedy after the event, when death or personal injury has already occurred. Financial compensation is a poor remedy for the loss of life, limbs, and dignity and for pain and suffering.

The real protection of rights is perhaps not the law, but is twofold—firstly, the individual patient's belief in his/her status and position and secondly, the recognition by health-care professionals that patients should be treated with respect, consideration and humanity and their autonomy recognised.

Both these factors are essential. Frequently the patient becomes institutionalised quickly, is prepared to give up all autonomy 'whatever you think doctor' and instances of the wrong patient being wheeled down to surgery because of a reluctance to challenge staff are not uncommon. Staff have difficulties respecting and deferring to those who have so little self-esteem.

On the other hand, professional standards of care, professional accountability and responsibility and professional acknowledgement of patients' rights are some of the most important forms of protection for the patient.

We should all recognise the sentiment expressed by Susan Sontag:

> "Illness is the night-side of life, a more onerous citizenship. Everyone who is born holds dual citizenship, in the kingdom of the well and in the kingdom of the sick. Although we all prefer to use only the good passport, sooner or later each of us is obliged at least for a spell, to identify ourselves as citizens of that other place."

It behoves us all, therefore, to recognise and protect the rights and responsibilities of the patients, for in so doing we are protecting ourselves.

Further reading

Allsop, J. *Health Policy and the National Health Services.* Longman 1984.

Beauchamp, T.L. and Childress, J.E. *Principles of Biomedical Ethics.* Oxford University Press 1989.

Brazier, M. *Medicines, Patients and the Law.* Penguin (2nd Ed.) 1992.

Cartwright, A. *Patients and their Doctors.* Routledge and Kegan Paul 1967.

Cohen, D.R. and Henderson, J. *Health Prevention and Economics* Oxford University Press 1988.

Dimond, B.C. *Legal Aspects of Nursing* Prentice Hall 1990.

Dimond, B.C. *Accountability. Managing Care Series.* Distance Learning Centre. University of the South Bank 1992.

Hepple and Matthews *Tort Cases and Materials.* Butterworths 1991

Illich *Medical Nemesis.* New York. Pantheon 1975

Jansen, A.R. *The New Medicine and the Old Ethics.* Harvard University Press 1990

Law Commission Consultation Paper No. 119. Decision Making and Mentally Incapacitated Adult. HMSO 1991.

Mason, J. and McCall, S. *Law and Medical Ethics.* Butterworths 1991.

Murphy, E. *After the Asylums* Faber & Faber 1991

Morgan, D. and Lee, R.G. *Human Fertilisation and Embryology Act 1990.* Blackstones 1991.

Rowson, R. *An Introduction to Ethics for Nurses.* Scutari Press 1991.

Townsend, P. (ed.) *Inequalities in health; The Black report.* Penguin 1982.

Tschudin, V. *Ethics in Nursing.* Heinemann 1991.

UKCC publications

Code of Professional Conduct for the Nurse, Midwife and Health Visitor. Revised Edition. 1992

Advisory Paper. Confidentiality: an elaboration of Clause 9 of the Second Edition of the UKCC's Code of Professional Conduct. April 1987.

Scope of Professional Practice. 1992.

White, R.; Carr, P. and Lowe, N. *A Guide to the Children Act 1989,* Butterworths 1990.

Reference could also be made to the service provided by Meditec from whom a bibliography of nursing books is available address: Meditec York House 26 Bourne Road Colsterworth Lincs. NG33 5JE tel. 0476 860281.

A wealth of articles on legal issues is available in almost all professional journals, and the practitioner should use these to keep up with recent cases and new legislation.

Glossary

AVMA	Association for the Victims of Medical Accidents.
Black Report	The report of the committee chaired by Sir D. Black on Inequalities in Health which reported in 1980. Reprinted in Townsend, P. and Davidson, N. *Inequalities in Health.* London: Penguin 1982.
Bolam Test	The test used by the courts to determine the standard of care in a case of alleged professional negligence.
Common law	Law which derives from decisions of judges in individual cases. Contrast with law laid down by statute. (see statutory)
CHC	Community Health Council
Detained Patients	Those detained under the provisions of the Mental Health legislation. (In England and Wales—Mental Health Act 1983.)
DMUs	Directly Managed Units, i.e. hospitals which are under the control of a health service authority and do which do not have independent trust status.
ECT	Electro-convulsive therapy
FHSA	Family Health Services Authority. Appointed by the Secretary of State as a statutory body to hold contracts with general practitioners, dentists, and pharmacists for the provision of NHS services within its district.
HA	Health Authority a statutory body appointed by the Secretary of State to manage health (hospital and Community services) within its district.
Health Service Commissioner	A person appointed to investigate complaints arising in the National Health Service. Sometimes known as the Ombudsman.
Iatrogenic	Illness/medical conditions caused by earlier medical treatment.
Internal market	A concept implemented following the NHS and Community Care Act 1990 that there should be purchasers and providers of health care within each district.

Legislation	Acts of Parliament (statutes) and statutory instruments which define the law.
Limitation of time	A defence which can be raised when the time limits set for bringing an action have been exceeded. See text for many exceptions to the time limits.
Plaintiff	The person who brings an action in the civil courts, usually for compensation.
Pleadings	The document which pass between the parties to a court action which sets out the claim and the defences and other particulars before the court hearing takes place. The aim is to identify the issues between the parties to reduce or even eliminate the need for hearing.
Practitioner	Term used to describe nurses, midwives, and health visitors.
Precedent	Ruling established by a court that may be binding upon courts hearing similar disputes at a later time. A hierarchy of courts determines which rulings are binding on subsequent court hearings.
Prima facie	At first sight. Phrase used to denote there would appear to be at a superficial level a possible legal action.
Provider	A health service body which agrees to contract to provide specific health services.
Purchaser	A health service body which contracts with a provider for specific health services to be provided.
QALY	Quality adjusted life years. A formula used by health economists to contrast the value of different forms of treatment. (Oregon, in the USA, made use of a similar scheme to determine priorities in the provision of health care.)
Statutory	Laid down by Act of Parliament. (Term often used to contrast with common law.)
Tort	A civil wrong (excluding breach of contract) and including negligence, nuisance, breach of a statutory duty, defamation which are actionable in the civil courts.
Trespass	An action which can be brought in the civil court alleging direct interference with lands, goods, or the person of the plaintiff.

UKCC   United Kingdom Central Council for Nursing, Midwifery and Health Visiting.

Index

N

National Health Service &
Community Care Act, 27, 63
National Health Service Act 1977,
7
Negligence, 16
NHS Trusts, 27
No-fault compensation scheme, 25

O

Occupational health
    Confidentiality in, 53
Ombudsman
    See Health Service Commissioner

P

Patient's Charter , 61
Patients' responsibilities, 5
Police and Criminal Evidence Act
1984, 50
Privacy
    Right to, 55
Private patients
    Responsibilities of, 75
Privileged information, 49

Q

QALY, 11

R

Research
    Informing participants in, 40
    Minors and, 35
Right to die, 32

S

Second opinion
    Right to, 54
Sexual relations
    Rights to, 56
Standard of care, 16
Suicide, 32
    Aiding and abetting, 32
Supply and demand, 11

T

Terminal illness
    Notification to patients of, 46
The Mental Health Act 1983, 55
The Pearson Report, 24
Trespass, 29

U

Unfair Contract Terms Act, 76

V

Vaccine Damages Payment Act
1979, 24
Visiting rules, 70